CITY COMFORTS

HOW TO BUILD AN URBAN VILLAGE

DAVID SUCHER

PHOTOGRAPHS BY DAVID SUCHER EXCEPT AS NOTED

SKETCHES BY KEVIN KANE

CITY COMFORTS PRESS
SEATTLE • 1995

THANK YOU

Many people made valuable suggestions about early drafts or simply helped by their conversation and I would like to thank them: Brian Dudgeon, Clair Enlow, Mark Hinshaw, Rich Untermann, Tony Puma, Gerry Johnson, Don Miles, Laurie Sucher, Julia Walton, David Wright, Donald K. Erickson, Marcia Wagoner, Michael Reed, Scott Flett. Some people read drafts with particularly active red pencils and I thank them, too: Fire Cruxent, Donald Padelford, Penelope Bell and John Davies.

In particular I would like to recognize Magrit Baurecht for graphic design, Alexander Zatko of Pine Tree Design for pre-press, Marilyn Meyer for editing and a parents'-eye view, and Barbara Gray for research assistance. I would like to especially thank Christopher K. Leman for his editing ideas and his very helpful conversation about transportation.

Many thanks to my special friend Elizabeth Kanny, without whose down-to-earth common sense this book would be titled something like *An Empirical Approach to Optimum Urban Development with Reference to Specific Elements of the Physical Infrastructure Conducive to Increased Social Interaction* and you would not be reading even this far.

Thanks also to a friend who pointed out—as I procrastinated about releasing the manuscript to the printer—that architects have an apt saying: *Better built than perfect.*

Second Printing 1996

Published by City Comforts
5605 Keystone Place North
Seattle, Washington 98103
(206) 545-4523
dsucher@citycomforts.com

FIRST WORDS

This book is not about any particular city. A good number of the photographs are in and about Seattle, Washington. But that's only because I live there. The photos are, by and large, simply *types*. In fact, better examples might very well exist in other cities (and I would appreciate knowing of them.)

A METAPHOR

CITY COMFORTS presents a metaphor—*the urban village*—as a way of describing the mix of intimacy and anonymity that I believe most people desire and which is largely missing in our large urban settlements.

A SHIFT IN FOCUS

This book is an attempt to refocus our public policy discussion from abstract generalities, colored maps and grandiose projects to the details that create our daily experience. It is about a way of looking at and speaking about our immediate environment.

NOT GLOBAL STRATEGY BUT HORSESHOES

Too much of our discussion is devoted to grand strategic visions. Certainly those are important. Whether or not we build more mass-transit systems or where we place a major public facility such as an airport are certainly decisions with long legs. And many regions are groping toward a grand *urban containment policy* to hold back urban sprawl and create denser cities through reweaving the tears in the urban fabric.

But no matter what the investment or the strategy, what is as important for the individual human being is the manner in which it works at the personal level. Small details at the individual scale are where a strategy is lost or won. The battle is forfeit if the horse is mis-shod.

TALK PRECEDES ACTION

This book emphasizes the importance of public and private conversation in creating the reality we have around us. In Homer the characters speak and describe what they will do before they do it. To take poetic license to Churchill, 'We build our cities first with words and then with bricks.'

THE SPECIFIC DETAILS

Most importantly, the book shows examples of small things—*city comforts*—that make urban life pleasant: places where people can meet, methods to tame cars and to make buildings good neighbors, art that infuses personality into *locations* and makes them into *places*.

Many of these small details are so obvious as to be invisible.

MY GOAL

I hope this book changes your way of looking at the city, or at the very least, provides a few hours' diversion and amusement.

CITY COMFORTS CONTENTS

EFFECTIVE CITY PLANNING RECOGNIZES THAT THIS FRAME OF MIND IS AT THE ROOT OF AMERICAN CULTURE.

How Seriously Should We Take the Phrase Urban Village?

You'd think that just as I'm about to launch into a book of 175 or so pages, I would urge splendid obeisance. Not so.

The very first mistake in creating comfortable cities would be to take the phrase too seriously. The term *urban village* is at heart a fragment of poetry. It's a metaphor and a matter of tone. It's a shorthand way of describing the *feel* we want from our cities. Certainly there are places that feel like an urban village and we can use them as benchmarks. But—belying the very subtitle of this book—we can't *build* urban villages in one fell swoop; we watch them evolve out of a multitude of individual actions over a long period of time.

The brilliance of the phrase is that it sums up our coexisting desire for autonomy and community. We want to have the quiet, tree-lined street with quick access to the global market. We desire a place of repose as well as a place of activity. This tension in human relations with the environment is an old one. The phrase urban village is simply a way of summing it up.

Its importance is as inspiration. Musicians use a little device called a pitch-pipe to help set the key in which to tune an instrument. Consider the term urban village as a place to begin tuning our communities so that they have a certain feel.

It would be hubris to think that one can take a map of a city and start to draw lines and say "Inside this line is an urban village."

For one thing, it's likely to scare people. "Another new government program. Bah!" And indeed, the self-perpetuating bureaucracies of government are just as likely to see an urban village as job security as to see it as an enjoyable place to live.

For another, interesting places grow and evolve out of the intelligence of thousands of people over many years. Little could be more destructive of the urban village vision than to think of it as a particular place, with a sharp boundary and a sign that announces "Here is Urban Village 000896FG. Built in 2001 by..."

What's important is to administer the rules and regulations of a city in the urban village *spirit*: slowly, carefully and over a long period of time. And with a sense of humor.

> **The very first mistake...would be to take the phrase too seriously.**

> **...administer the rules and regulations of a city in the urban village spirit...And with a sense of humor.**

HOW TO BUILD AN URBAN VILLAGE

A MAYOR'S PHRASE

Not very long ago, the mayor of Seattle—Norm Rice—was speaking to our City Council about planning. In an offhand and casual way, he suggested that henceforth the city's planning would aim to build *urban villages.* It was genuinely a throwaway line and buried deep in his talk. But the response was galvanic. The phrase captivated people. It was seized upon. It struck a chord. It brought attention well beyond original expectation.

The urban village phrase called forth an article in *The New York Times,* where Seattle planning is hardly local news. The Mayor, a good listener, made the phrase a central part of his administration's planning efforts.

At the time I was a member of Seattle's Planning Commission. Our reaction was: "Urban Village. Hmmm.. What a great idea. It's brilliant. We like it. We're all in favor. Sounds great!" Then we turned to each other and scratched our heads and asked "What's an urban village?"

AN OXYMORON

At first glance the term might seem to be nonsensical and impossible: an oxymoron, the two words contradict each other. How can you have a place that feels like a village and a big city at the same time? The village is small, intimate, quiet; one knows the other villagers and may even be related to them. The city is big, busy, diverse and filled with strangers. Life can be lonely in the big city. So what was the Mayor talking about? What is this urban village?

NOT BRAND NEW

The phrase *urban village* was not a new one. Sociologist Herbert Gans had spoken of urban villagers in the book by the same name when he studied the lives of first generation Italian immigrants in Boston. Though these people lived in the great and urbane metropolis, their lives were bounded and limited as if they still lived in their native peasant villages.

But in Seattle the urban villagers now contemplated and proposed wore penny-loafers, not peasant boots.

Some farseeing planners from Australia, and even the Prince of Wales, more recently used the phrase to describe a new (or old, as it were) form of city characterized by neighborhoods with few cars but dynamic mixes of housing, shops and offices and by, in the Prince's words, 'human scale, intimacy...vibrant street life.'

BUT PROVOCATIVE AND POETIC

What is so provocative and allusive about these two words? Why has there been such a popular response?

One thought is that the phrase is poetry, or at least a fragment of a poem, a pair of trochee: (*"A metrical foot consisting of one long or stressed syllable followed by one short or unstressed syl-*

lable. ") It gains some of its power from its rhythm.

A Phrase of Contradiction

But most importantly, it is the contradiction that makes the phrase interesting. It conjures two different forms of settlement (and their associated emotions) and brings them cheek-by-jowl. As political rhetoric it calls for the creation of a city of contrary sensations. It is a metaphor of unusual power.

Urban	Village
hustle-bustle	tranquility
liberty	structure
lonely	together
hostile	friendly
far away	close by
strangers	kindred
possibilities	limits
growth	stasis
artificial	natural
complex	simple
large	small
skyscraper	cottage
liberal	conservative
anonymous	familiar

The words—*urban* and *village*— are filled with opposing emotions, reflecting our feelings about each environment. The phrase drew attention and praise because people want to feel both sensations. We want to live in a city which is intimate enough so that our face is well-known and respected by our local police officer. But we also want to have the privacy to make friends with people of which our parents might not approve. We want familiarity *and* anonymity.

People Want Both

Both scales of settlement have flaws. People want the best of both worlds: the diversity, choice and independence of the *Urb* and the homeyness and intimacy of the *Village.*

Upon reflection, it seemed quite possible that urban village was a metaphor for a certain kind of city and a certain kind of relaxed relationship among people. As a Planning Commissioner, I believed that the term urban village—by its unique and poetic character—was itself setting forth a challenge to create a city in which we have the best of both environments: the great diversity of the city and the familiarity of a village.

The political and practical challenge is to translate these two feelings —*urban* and *village*—into real streets and real buildings.

But before you can build an urban village, you have to know what it is and how to recognize one.

How to Recognize an Urban Village

Here is one urban village indicator: While you are driving around a modern American city you come across a commercial district where you want to get out of your car and stroll around; you have found an urban village, ...or at least a potential one.

Putting it another way, if you pass right by a parking lot and retail strip-center without the slightest inclination to stop, because it does not appear *interesting*, you have *not* passed an urban village.

SANTA BARBARA, CALIFORNIA

of physical objects: of houses and streets, of parks and stores. But the real importance of a neighborhood, at least to me, is that it is made of neighbors. Neighborhoods would be a pointless *non sequitur* without neighbors. It's not the buildings *per se* that make a neighborhood. It's the neighbors. It's the *neighborliness.*

AND WHO ARE NEIGHBORS?

Neighbors are not simply people who live in physical proximity. Neighbors are people who are acquainted with each other, at least by sight. Neighbors have some sense of human connection. Neighbors recognize and acknowledge each other, if at least with a nod of the head. Neighbors have some sense of responsibility to each other. Neighbors are not anonymous. Neighbors may even have a drink together.

Although this book shows buildings and streets and other hardware, the real focus is not on physical objects but on human relations. The effort to create an *urban village* in physical form is only a means to an end. The means are buildings and roads and parks. The end is improving relations between people.

To a large degree, the future urban villages will emerge out of our existing neighborhoods. So it's of critical importance that we identify those things about our neighborhoods which we value and want to preserve. Let's look at that issue a little more.

WHAT'S A NEIGHBORHOOD?

For a starter, what's a neighborhood? Obviously, it's a collection

CARMEL, CALIFORNIA

Consider some words on the neck label of Bert Grant's *Celtic Ale*—words written to be read and contemplated slowly, bottle in hand—(and by the way, a very nice ale):

Great ale makes great times. Great times make great friends. Great friends make great neighborhoods. Great neighborhoods make great cities. Great cities make great nations. Great nations make a great world. Therefore, the greatness of the world depends on ale. And Celtic Ale is one of the world's great ales. And only I make it. — Bert Grant

NECK LABEL FROM CELTIC ALE

PART OF THE ANSWER IS ARCHITECTURAL

The patterns and ideas shown in this book are part of the answer, yet architecture and urban design is simply *one* tool. The good news is that design that promotes community is not a task for rocket scientists; and you'll see some of the basics in a moment.

There are many details to observe in cities and in these pictures but the reader might focus on and consider, above all, *the placement of the buildings in relation to the sidewalk.*

Simple as it may be, this relationship of the building to the sidewalk is one of the key architectural decisions in city planning for cohesive neighborhoods. This relationship is significant

LOS ANGELES, CALIFORNIA

in residential areas but is of supreme importance in commercial areas. Indeed, it is the position of the building with respect to the sidewalk which makes a city.

The good news is that the relationship is a very simple one: place the building at the sidewalk. That's it. Don't make it complicated. Just bring the building to the sidewalk. If you question this, consider the places that most people like to go on vacation: New York, Paris, London, Aspen, Carmel, Nantucket, Park City, Friday Harbor and even Disneyland! Every last one of them is built so that the building comes right up to the sidewalk.

Historically, this is quite understandable. With only human and animal power to move goods, and with market forces in charge, it made sense to bring the building as close to the right-of-way as possible. In fact, oftentimes the building would cantilever out over the street in the effort to maximize profit, creating, ironically for modern preservationists, the most charming streets.

SOME DEVELOPERS KNOW THE RULES

People who make ersatz cities also understand that this spatial relationship is central to our sense of being in a city. There is a very interesting tourist attraction at Universal Studios in Los Angeles. It is called *City Walk* and it is a festival shopping center, a place to shop for things one doesn't need.

Of course it has valet parking—wonderfully ironic here—which is *de rigueur* in Los Angeles. It combines both status and security: the uniformed attendants running to-and-fro to fetch cars ensure that anyone else in the garage stands out by their presence alone.

CITY WALK, LOS ANGELES, CALIFORNIA

The fascinating thing about *City Walk* is that its developers understood one essence of city, what brings in the customers: it is buildings that come up to sidewalks where people can stroll and shop safely. This mall—even more than most malls—has the basic village pattern: the old village sidewalk! While many developers seem to have an aversion to cities, they also recognize that people are drawn to city-like situations and will drive to find them.

CITY WALK, LOS ANGELES, CALIFORNIA

THREE CRUCIAL PATTERNS

Three important patterns will emerge over and over again in the pictures and their importance cannot be overemphasized; they are the common denominator and *leit motiv* of comfortable urban spaces. While by themselves insufficient, they are an absolute necessity and precursor to creating communities. Let me say that again: By themselves these certain architectural relationships are not enough to create healthy communities. There are unhealthy inner-city neighborhoods that have them and auto-dominated—but healthy—suburbs that don't. But as a general rule the following patterns are essential to create the human settlements that have any real sense of interpersonal community.

RULE # 1
BUILD TO THE SIDEWALK

First, notice how the buildings almost always come right up to the sidewalk, which in the vast majority of cases is the property line.

As we said before, this pattern is central, and to paraphrase Professor Strunk (of *The Elements of Style)* whose desire to eliminate useless words left him repeating the useful ones for emphasis:

"Build to the sidewalk!
Build to the sidewalk!
Build to the sidewalk!"

The sidewalk is important because it channels pedestrian movements

SAN FRANCISCO, CALIFORNIA

and forces people into closer proximity where they may bump into each other and act neighborly.

RULE #2
MAKE THE STREETFRONT PERMEABLE

Then, please notice that the photos always show storefronts that you can see into and out of. Life attracts life. If you can't see the merchandise for sale or the other patrons mingling, you won't stop to go in. It's a basic rule of retailing and practical urban design the

TOKYO, JAPAN

world over. Flaunt it. Show it. Don't hide it with a blank wall! Place windows and openings along the sidewalk.

Of course, not only must people be able to see in and out, they must also be able to enter. Therefore put your front doors where they are visible from and directly face the sidewalk.

Such opening of the building to the sidewalk is a common denominator of all healthy neighborhoods and potential urban villages.

PORTLAND, OREGON

RULE #3
PUT THE PARKING BEHIND, OR UNDER, OR ABOVE OR TO THE SIDE OF THE BUILDING

Parking lots are a necessity. But unless you are in high school, or are at a tailgate party before a football game, or at a classic car *concours d'elegance*, parking lots are not the kind of place you want to hang around. It is so ironic, of course: we invest such great money and emotion in our cars and yet we don't want to hang around them in parking lots!

VANCOUVER, B.C.

Parking lots are crucial but *taming* them will be one of the crucial parts of piecing-together urban villages.

...the basic rule must be to put the parking out of sight.

In an urban village, there are no parking lots along the streetfront. This is the corollary of the rule that asks for the buildings to be brought to the sidewalk. But since it's so important (and so simple) it bears repeating: put the parking behind the building and place the building at the sidewalk: save the front for people.

Now this is a very simple rule but, alas, in reality easier said than done. The reality is that in our car-oriented culture, there are situations in which we want the parking very close at hand. The typical strip-center approach—put the parking in front of the building—is hard to avoid if you want it to serve people late at night. Talk as we might about proper urban design, no one is going to feel comfortable going to a 7-11 at 2 AM and walking around from the back of the building to the entrance. It's bad enough when the parking is in front—in the dark of night it is not an inviting choice. The basic rules of feeling safe—natural surveillance and territoriality—are at work in the conventional strip-center development. But while the principle may work for the one site, the same pattern, repeated over and over, is counterproductive to safety as it creates a neighborhood of a scale where people only want to be in cars.

Luckily, there are very few uses such as the 24-hour convenience store where access at odd hours must be a design constraint. Certainly safety, safety through the eyes of others, is essential. But the idea that parking must be in front of the shop, right off the sidewalk, would be designing a city around a worst-case situation. It would create a city designed around the need to go to a convenience store for a six-pack at 2 A.M.! So the basic rule must be to put the parking out of sight.

Of course there will be some times when it's difficult to meet this rule.

Therefore, below is an example to demonstrate that alternatives to parking lots between the street and the storefront do exist.

COMFORT: MEASURE OF AN URBAN VILLAGE

Following "man is the measure of the world," so, now "human comfort is the measure of a city's success."

My own experience with local government is as a staff-member, citizen and real estate developer and I believe our society makes the problem of city building far too complicated. We confuse it with grandeur and we confuse it with complex public administration. It is neither. The main task is making people comfortable, the same task faced by the host at a party. In fact, think of the main job for the City Planner as being the Amy Vanderbilt of the city.

All around us are examples of excellence in concept and design: city comforts. They are simple to recognize, simple to explain and, by and large, simple to build. These designs-that-work can be repeated many times before, if ever, they run thin. This book is dedicated to showing them.

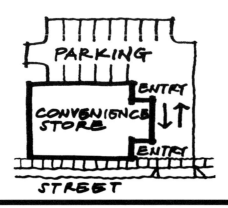

SOME OVER-RIDING PRINCIPLES
ABOVE ALL, ATTEND TO DETAILS

Details count. The comfortable city and the urban village are both built and experienced as a series of details, which may appear seamless and coherent, if things work well, but in fact were created over a lengthy period of time and by a variety of minds. Although a building may be very large, we perceive it detail-by-detail. An ordinary, even banal structure, can and will be transformed into a marvel if the designer and builder have thought through the users' needs and reflect those needs in details.

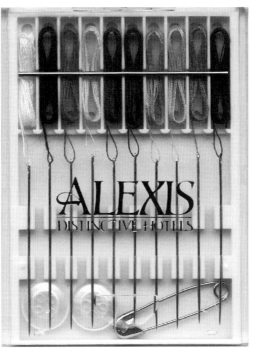

The sewing kit pictured here is from a hotel in Portland, Oregon and is a striking example of forethought and consideration. The harried traveler, late for a meeting in a distant part of a strange city, who has lost a button, is saved the further vexation of threading the needle (the eye of which seems to become smaller and smaller with each passing year) by this sewing kit with *pre-threaded needles.*

This humble sewing kit embodies a respect for details. It is an approach to doing things which can be applied to automobiles, VCRs and to the built environment. It is a mindset, an approach to reality, a manner of seeing things or not seeing things, which is of crucial strategic importance if we are to build comfortable cities. It is a mindset which is devoted to quality, to refinement, to paying attention to details. It is a mindset missing to some strong degree in most of our country. We are struggling to produce excellent products for the global economy for some of the same reasons that we are struggling to create comfortable cities: we pay insufficient attention to the details. It is a cliche, and therefore at least partly true, that "God is in the details." But of course, so is the devil.

The novelist Michael Crichton explains this approach in a recent novel.

Two Americans are examining a new VCR made in Japan.

> "...Very neat. So small." He turned to me, holding up the box. "You know how the Japanese can make things this way and we can't? They *kaizen* 'em. A process of deliberate, patient, continual refinement. Each year the products get a little better, a little cheaper. Americans don't think that way. Americans are always looking for the quantum leap, the big advance forward. Americans try to hit a home run—to knock it out of the park—and then sit back. The Japanese hit singles all day long, and they never sit back. So with something like this, you're looking at an expression of philosophy as much as anything."

Or, in other words, and paraphrasing the architect Mies van der Rohe:

> "God *and profit* is in the details."

MONKEY SEE, MONKEY DO
COPY THE SUCCESSFUL

The lessons drawn in this book are not new. Most have been known for hundreds or even thousands of years, and they were often better understood then.

Don't bother with *originality*. If you've got enormous talent, it will show; otherwise the quest for the *novel* for its own sake can be just a form of self-advertising.

We are all copycats at heart. It's the way we learn as children and the way we learn as adults. Except as adults we approach it a little more systematically (at times) and call it reverse engineering. Most of our business culture operates in such a copycat manner: see who is doing well, analyze the whys and

'...back-out' the specific rules that make them successful.

hows, and then, to the degree allowed by the law (and obviously, sometimes beyond), do it the same way.

Our culture of building—particularly the regulatory process—could and should operate more as reverse engineering than it does. As urban planners we must find details of the environment about which there is general agreement, back-out the specific rules that make them successful and write the zoning codes to favor such patterns.

CITY COMFORTS
ARE IN PUBLIC

City comforts are small things of the urban landscape and, to a very large degree, involve the way the building meets the street, or the street itself, or things which can be seen from the street.

Thus, there are no hot tubs under a gazebo on an estate in Beverly Hills here. It is what happens at the private/public edge that makes an urban village and the focus of this book.

Choose an Appropriate Standard of Review

Our expectations for buildings should be modest and realistic. And such realism starts with the perspective—the standard of review—that we use to evaluate new buildings in our landscape.

We are too harsh on our architects and builders. We somehow expect each new work to be novel and full of surprise. This point–of–view does not help to create amiable cities. It looks at the wrong things. People—architects included—often speak of a building and decry it as *derivative* or *nothing special*. When questioned further, they will readily admit that the building isn't bad, really, but it's not a "great work."

To wonder if a particular building is a great work is to hold it up to a flawed standard of review on two counts.

First, such an approach tends to overemphasize the purely visual; one examines the building as if it were a photograph on a wall and one talks of balance and composition and so on.

Secondly, the very nature of the question asks one to view the building as a discrete object—isolated on its own lot—not as a piece of a city landscape.

Both aspects play into the misuse—albeit ancient—of architecture as a tool of social aggrandizement, posturing and pomposity. Such an attitude may feed the hungry maw of the architecture and design press but it does little to nourish the eye or body of the would–be urban villager.

The *great work* standard is out–of-scale. Something more modest is needed.

More often than not, the important question is not whether some particular building is a great building. The correct standard of review is more this:

"If this building were just about standard for the community, would we still want to live here?"

Be realistic. Does the building follow the very few basic rules of urban design? If so, grant the permit and build it.

Of course every town needs a few memorable structures of civic pride and joy: a stadium, a tower, a church or temple. But these are by practical necessity few; the majority of buildings will be (we hope) good, solid, money-making background buildings. It is only occasionally that a building—by special use or unique site—needs to be a focal point. Our cities have a long way to go before it's appropriate to use the great work standard of architectural review for everything.

Let's redefine our standard of greatness so that striving and self-promotion are excluded.

> **Both aspects play into the misuse—albeit ancient—of architecture as a tool of social aggrandizement, posturing and pomposity**

BACK BAY, BOSTON, MASSACHUSETTS

LET USES OVERLAP: HOUSES AND SHOPPING

Because of its scale, the urban village will have a mixture of uses within close walking distance of each other— or even down a flight of stairs. But most contemporary land-use laws focus on buffering weaker uses from the impacts of stronger and incompatible uses. There are many common sense reasons for such zoning of uses. These concerns are antique. The Mesopotamians, for example, forbade metal workers from plying their trade within cities because of danger from fire and smoke.

Since the late 19th century it has been planners' progressive gospel to separate uses, particularly residential and commercial uses. The gentler and quieter residential districts should be protected from the busier commercial and industrial uses. Up to a point this separation makes sense. But taken to an extreme it has led to vast monocultures of uses.

Natural ecosystems are richest at their edges where different habitats and their associated species overlap. Mixed-use neighborhoods are often more resilient, stimulating and interesting than single-use neighborhoods. Hybrid vigor is recognized in agronomy; mixture of uses can also impart vigor to social communities.

There are conflicting activities in natural systems and some users win out over time. So too in human systems. Some uses do conflict with each other— housing wants quiet; shopping thrives on bustle. But they can coexist close

NORTH VANCOUVER, B.C.

together if their conflict points are identified. We can separate parking areas for residential and commercial tenants in mixed-use buildings to diminish noise and security problems.

Of course the single-family neighborhood will continue to be the staple of settlement through the foreseeable future. But even in single-family residential areas, certain low-key commercial uses can mix-in very well and add vitality, economic stability and safety.

LET USES OVERLAP: SHOPS AND TRANSPORT

Another place to mix uses is at transportation hubs. What could be more logical than putting daily shopping where you change mode of transport? It's an obvious convenience and it makes taking public transit more feasible because it saves time. Instead of taking the bus home and then driving to shop, one can shop in the course of returning from work.

Applaud Good Work with Precision

The most basic phrase of good manners is "Thank you." The most effective way to receive an encore or repeat performance is to shower the actor with applause. Positive reinforcement is the basis of behavior modification in either education or business. As a society, we do that far too rarely and with little aplomb. Of course we applaud with money, that is, by buying someone's product. It would help to add this basic tool of good management—thanks and recognition—to the governmental land-use arsenal.

Behind those real estate signs and partnerships there are persons. In fact, the real estate development business is singularly entrepreneurial; many sizable operations are the domain of a very few individuals. Like everyone else, they are motivated by more than just money. When developers do good work, show them that we citizens care and explain *very specifically* what they have done right so that all will understand how things work, in an urban design sense.

With real estate developers, as with pets and children, it is important to reward good behavior immediately upon its heels. Otherwise, being unconnected in time, the reward will not relate to a specific action. The reward must be timely, and specific, and must explain precisely what *works* about the project or element.

Keystone Building, Seattle

Urban Cabin™ Condominiums

a True Tale

Dave: You know, Don, our buyers will like our new urban cabins because these condominiums will be distinguished by their superb dynamic spatial continuity as well as by a component massing which proposes a four-dimensional interplay of those precise yet amorphous elements which are essential to the creation of an appropriate urban contextualism in the late 20th century.

Don: Oh! For God's sake, David! Cut the B.S. and just tell 'em that they're good-looking, well-built, and cheap.

SEATTLE

USE SMALL WORDS TO DISCUSS THE LANDSCAPE

Our buildings respond to our conversation about the urban landscape—from zoning codes to breakfast chat. A comfortable city needs a populace which cares about the built environment, knows what it wants and has the vocabulary.

But archi-babble—like kudzu—has a way of creeping in and taking over any real conversation about the built environment by channelling conversation into a display of fancy *concepts* rather than individual *feelings*. We defeat our own goal of comfortable cities when we use words that confuse the citizens, who should be able and confident to speak with feeling, perception and precision about the landscape around them. Of course some technical terms are useful shorthand, but such compression can also act like jargon and like any jargon, can limit important conversation to a self-selecting elite. But the city is a social work and all must take part.

> **We defeat our own goal of comfortable cities when we use words that confuse the citizens.**

To promote widespread discussion of the city landscape, use small words.

Do Simple Things Now

There is a rule of science known as "Occam's razor," most often attributed to a 14th century monk, William of Occam. The rule states, in essence, that when there are several alternative explanations for a natural phenomenon, we should choose the explanation which has the fewest and least complex assumptions.

There should be a corollary notion for city planning. We should choose the simplest and most economical means of solving a problem rather than the most complex and expensive. But how seldom we do so. Particularly now that we have established remarkable systems of transport, power, and communications, it is time to consolidate our gains and attend to fine-tuning these systems.

Many athletic trainers believe that the origin of high performance is in simple things such as good breathing. Similarly, the majority of golf professionals will tell you that the origin of a graceful, efficient and comfortable swing is in the two things you do before you even start the swing itself: how you *grip* the club and how you *stand* when facing the ball.

Why do we constantly seek the more difficult path? For example, rather than facing the reality of the *personal vehicle*—that term raises fewer hackles than *automobile*—and taming it, we spend our time arguing about and then building expensive systems, either rail or road. Rather than fix the leaky roof with the many traffic calming devices available, or a vastly improved bus system (which could be developed incrementally), we would prefer to build a brand new house. The question is more for students of group psychology and organizational dynamics than urban planning and architecture; the answer lies more in personal ambition than common sense or public interest.

But, fighting against the trends as it may be, do simple things now.

Rather than fix the leaky roof, we would prefer to build a brand new house.

How to use this Book

This book offers workable responses to typical problems of the urban landscape. It's obviously neither a text book nor an encyclopedia. It's a personal statement of what one person has observed and believes to be important. It's not meant to be a complete or systematic study.

So, other than the simply curious, there are four groups of people who may benefit from this book.

Neighbors

Neighbors could use this book to talk with developers and tinker with projects. More often than not, neighbors are at a loss to effectively deal with developers. They often approach new development with a very *not-in-my-backyard* attitude. Though they may claim the high moral ground of speaking for "the community," little conversation is needed to see that some, at least, are out to protect their own vested interests—the on-street parking space in front of their own house, for example—as much as any developer.

Neighbors too often start from a viewpoint—more accurate as an exception than as the rule—that development can actually be stopped. Our system of local government taxation and administration is biased in favor of development. Fairly often, neighbors have attempted to stop a project and ended up with high legal bills and a project exactly or virtually the same as first proposed.

More productive would be an approach which—grudgingly but realistically—accepts impending change but attempts to mold it into a form more civil and comfortable. It would be more productive for neighbors to go to a developer and say something like: "Look. We're not really happy about any change in our neighborhood and we're not sure how far we will go in contesting you. But perhaps if you would change this aspect of the building here and that aspect there, we might see it differently."

Many an otherwise awful building would be quite acceptable if the developer had been encouraged to attend to the details and been aided with examples.

ARCHITECTS

Architects can use this book in talking to clients and showing them possibilities that work and that may increase the attractiveness and profitability of their project, as well as speeding the permitting process, which is another form of coin.

MUNICIPAL OFFICIALS

Administrators, too, might use the book to communicate with project proponents and opponents to show them ways that a project might be made to work better. People learn best and quickest when shown models and examples of things that have already worked for others.

PROPERTY OWNERS

The creation of comfortable environments can be a rewarding endeavor, both financially and psychically. It is private initiative that will create the environments of the future. Thus, it is on the outlook of the property developer that most of our effort should be placed. That guidance from governmental authority may be necessary is obvious, but unless we want to live in a police state, we must recognize that government cannot be everywhere, and that we must rely on the property owners' own inclinations. That is not to say that the property owners are not to be bounded, but the boundaries should be based on cultural expectations, not only government rules.

But the very best (and original) argument for zoning and land use regulations is the *preservation and enhancement of value* and it is that kind of argument that property owners will listen to. The designs shown here will increase the value of property by making it more attractive in the very broadest sense.

BUMPING INTO PEOPLE

BUMPING INTO PEOPLE

Cities are about bumping into and running into old and new friends. Or they should be. The city's job is to bring people together.

Early cities started as trade hubs, military centers, or religious shrines; cities still flourish for similar reasons. For each, the city provides a place of contact. The city is a place to make a business deal, enact rules and regulations, make friends and even fall in love. The city is a place to communicate——in all its facets.

But our cities work far below their potential. They fail to encourage the unplanned and serendipitous encounter upon which business grows. The possibility of the accidental meeting is what makes the city a fertile place. From the chance conversation springs the new business idea, and the lead for a new deal. People position themselves in cities so as to be able to make contacts with others of common interest.

Modern cities work even less well for pleasure. As Christopher Alexander put it, cities are a mechanism for "sustaining human contact." He goes on:

> People come to cities for contact. That's what cities are: meeting places. Yet the people who live in cities are often contactless and alienated. A few of them are physically lonely: almost all of them live in a state of endless inner loneliness. They have thousands of contacts, but the contacts are empty and unsatisfying.

The possibility of the accidental meeting is what makes the city a fertile place.

People flee cities because the cities do not do a good job as places where casual contact can flourish and create a sense of community. The modern city falls short in providing environments for communication. Sociologist Ray Oldenburg calls these environments *third places* in his book *The Great Good Place*. He describes the first two places as the home and the workplace. The third place is where one bumps into friends and neighbors in an unplanned manner. Such a place is a public place: the bar, the pub, the tavern, the coffee shop, the deli. Food or drink is essential; so is proximity to the home. But modern America is short of such places.

Ponder the TV show *Cheers* which takes place in a tavern of the same name. Its theme song fondly and plaintively describes the tavern as a place "where everybody knows your name." It speaks volumes about our current civilization that a place where one is recognized as an individual is something worth mentioning in a popular song.

We speak constantly of neighborhoods and community. But without the third place—the commons outside the home and workplace where people stumble into each other and where your name is known—we do not have a *neighborhood* but simply an *area*.

Of course public authorities should not and will not go into the tavern business. But the following principles can help create public places more conducive to meeting people, and they are courtesies which should be no surprise to the Amy Vanderbilts of the city:

PROVIDE SEATS

A seat is an explicit invitation to stay, either with others...

CANNON BEACH, OREGON

MALIBU BEACH, CALIFORNIA

SANTA BARBARA, CALIFORNIA

...or by oneself.

Unfortunately, because of concern that the wrong people, i.e. *street people,* will be the ones to use public seats, too often such seats are removed. It would be naive to assert that some street people present no problem; and it would be heartless to deny any social responsibility for the truly homeless. The wise social policy about them is far beyond the scope of this book. But certainly, removing public seating does not solve the problem but only denies the rest of the population its due of an inviting city.

LET PEOPLE PURCHASE FOOD OR DRINK

It seems inevitable that people at almost every party will end up in the kitchen. Oh perhaps not at the White House or the Elysée Palace, but at pretty much every party where they feel comfortable, they'll end up in the kitchen around the food. The same

St. Helena, California

principle applies in public: food relaxes, and a good meal is always the start to a seduction or a contract or a peace agreement. "Let us break bread together."

Even at a mountain resort, people like to hang around the food.

OFFER A CONVERSATION PIECE

Every host and hostess knows that it's nice to have some odd objects lying about for people to notice, exclaim over and discuss. It's best if the object is a souvenir from the last trip to Paris or Tibet, but it really doesn't

BLACK BUTTE RANCH, OREGON

NEFERTITI BEACH, GREEN RIVER, UTAH

matter. The purpose is to divert attention from I and Thou and to place it on some external object. Third parties are always popular as a subject, but we call that gossip and that's risky for strangers (not knowing who is who).

In public places, as on the beach, art engages people and will always do nicely to help open a conversation by providing an external object on which to focus.

DO IT DISCREETLY

Fostering social interaction is difficult and an overly enthusiastic or match–making host or hostess can be the surest way to spoil a burgeoning conversation. ("You two will love each other: you have so much in common!" or "Aren't we all having fun!!?")

CAUTION TO PLANNERS

Be limited in your goals. Creating community—which is what all this boils down to—is a worthy goal. But it is a goal largely beyond the reach of government.

Community evolves from individual conversations. Venues for these conversations are difficult to create. That's one reason very few adults ever hang around the so-called Community Center. Such places, built and managed by bureaucracy, most often fall flat. Necessarily run by gray government, they lack the unique and quirky personality often contributed by individual enterprise. Interesting public spaces provide only a framework, with the daily details supplied by aware entrepreneurs who recognize what is working and what is not, and act immediately.

ENCOURAGE THE CHANCE ENCOUNTER

Chance encounter. It could be the name of a movie from the '30s. But it is the most basic work of a city. Many interesting things happen to us because we bump into someone by accident: new projects, clients, and love affairs. Cities—and the marketplace is the first and still prime example—provide a venue for these serendipitous and accidental meetings. The city gives us the opportunity to *plan* to be in a place where *accidents* can happen, where we can run into others.

VANCOUVER, B.C.

But with the development of an electronic cyberspace will we still need cities? "We'll all do our work in front of our console from our home office," is a current cliche. And even if we don't work at home, maybe we will shop from there. Will physical proximity still be needed? Has the purpose of the city vanished in a flood of electrons? Will the virtual office and virtual store via Internet replace fixed ones?

The answer depends on the type of activity. Obviously, it will be very difficult for people in crafts such as tile or concrete to work in cyberspace.

For information workers the answer depends on whether cyberspace allows the opportunity for bumping into each other. Cities continue to grow because they still provide enormous possibility for the chance encounter. If advances in the quality of electronic communication allow the accidental meeting, then the imperative to place ourselves in physical proximity will diminish. In the traditional office the watercooler is the place where we meet accidentally. The virtual office will succeed when there is a *virtual watercooler.*

But the digital world evolves rapidly and will allow richer contact—well beyond mere words on screen—and the chance meeting on cyberspace may actually become a vibrant experience. Here is a challenge for the purpose of large-scale settlement. Cities successful in facing this challenge will recognize the importance of social interaction and chance meetings to economic growth. In every possible way: from convention centers to the design of sidewalks, cities which are designed to be sociable will be at an advantage in the economy of the future.

The virtual office will succeed when there is a virtual watercooler.

Build Neighborhoods for the Social Stroll

People like to walk together.

In many parts of the world, particularly the Latin nations it is a part of daily life to take an evening stroll. There is a complex and involved ritual to this walk, this promenade, this *passaggiaeta* or *paseo*, as it's called in Italy and Spain. It was a tradition in France and Britain, and in the United States, too, before the automobile spread us so far apart that one has to drive to find a place to walk.

Certain groups only walk with each other; men walk in some manner, women in another perhaps, children, teenagers and the very old in yet more ways. It all depends on the specific town and its customs. The stroll starts and stops with invisible but predictable regularity. The *passaggiaeta* is good for the health but it is more a social exercise than anything else. Chatting, watching other people, and being watched, are the reasons for the social stroll.

In the U.S. we have teenage *cruising* in cars. Older people use the shopping malls for their promenade. The stroll is a universal custom and impulse, though an impulse largely thwarted by the design of our American cities.

But suppose one had the opportunity to lay out a new town or merely a new suburban subdivision or perhaps just revitalize a shopping district and wished to meet the demand of future residents to take part in this ancient tradition. How would one proceed?

To a remarkable degree, we do have that opportunity. Suburban development still proceeds apace and there are many, many plats and new towns now on the drawing boards, so there is plenty of chance to do things differently and more traditionally.

Here are a few rules for walkways suited to the social stroll.

• *Continuity*: Create a path which forms a continuous loop, such as around a square or a small pond. People of all ages generally prefer to walk in a loop which gives a sense of departure and arrival. Furthermore, it is important that the route be clear, routine and "automatic" enough so that decisions about which way to turn are unneeded and hence can never interrupt the conversation.

• *Length*: The path must not be too lengthy so that people may pass each other more than once. Flirting can't be hurried. One must be able to make eye contact, remake it and then remake it again in order for the social contact to take root.

• *Width*: Since people like to stroll together, it would be ideal for the path to be wide enough for two groups to pass each other without awkward rearrangements to interrupt the conversation.

Watching other people, and being watched, and chatting, is the core of the social stroll.

Nantucket, Massachusetts

THIRD AVENUE, SEATTLE, PHOTO BY FRED HOUSEL

PUT PUBLIC SPACE IN THE SUN

The sun is the prime mover and the source of all life on earth. Though there is science fiction speculation that life might be able to evolve with another energy source, and in the absence of solar radiation, we are still earthlings, and we are all drawn to the sun.

Thus, if you would like a public plaza to be used, place it on a side of the building where it will receive sun. This may seem elementary, and it is, and too

simple to need stating, which it isn't, for it is still quite often ignored.

Better to have too much sun than too little. Shade may be needed in extreme climates, or for a few days a year in the temperate zones. But it can be provided with awnings and trellises. It is much more difficult to bend the sun around the building to its north side if that's where you placed the plaza.

Put Your Cards (or Chess Pieces) on the Table

People like the inherent amusement and challenge of board and table games. They are simply engaging and fun. But such distractions are a staple of culture for a deeper reason: they allow easy and nonthreatening socializing, with the enormous exception of the temptation to cheat. But cheating aside, card and board games provide an opportunity to be with people for hours and hours, actually enjoying their company, with nary a word of consequence ever spoken. There is no obligation to make conversation, or worse, to become ensnared in a pointless and unpleasant argument on politics, religion, money, sex or any of the other aspects of life which are so interesting and yet which can divide us most disagreeably.

CANNON BEACH, OREGON

BUILD CLOSE TO THE SIDEWALK

One of the benefits of smaller scale is that conversation is encouraged simply by physical proximity. People don't have to raise their voices if they are sitting close to the sidewalk.

Not incidentally, it's good for business; the power of suggestion can work on the passerby who sees customers enjoying what they have bought.

This scale is often called *human-scale*. What does that mean?

One useful definition of human-scale is a functional one. For example: an apartment building in which a child on the sidewalk can converse with his/her mother at a window up above. *That* is human-scale: a place where the ability to have a conversation is allowed by the very size of the space.

Note: The small town in Oregon where I took this picture has approximately *eighty* benches in its four blocks of main street. That's seating for about five hundred people: a superb seating-to-sidewalk ratio. It is a *very* comfortable town.

999 SECOND AVENUE, SEATTLE, PHOTO BY FRED HOUSEL

PROVIDE A PLACE FOR MUSIC

These entry steps to a major office building work in several ways. Of course, access to the building is their first function. They also act as a viewpoint to observe the passing scene.

But their circular shape also creates a small amphitheater and a place for performance, particularly music. Concerts at noon (called the *Out-to-Lunch* series) add music to daily life. Music provides the pleasure of sound.

It is an unobtrusive way to bring people together. It soothes. It helps us wile away boring times. It is an ancient pathway to religious and community experience.

This small space is close to but off the main pedestrian traffic pattern. Musicians (either *street* or *school*) can play here without disturbing those who pass by on the sidewalk but do not care to stop to listen.

RECLAIM & PEOPLE THE PARKING LOT

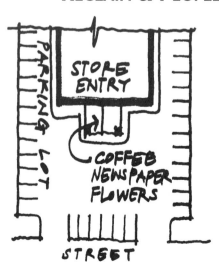

The entrance to a supermarket is an ideal place to sell potted plants and cut flowers. It is also ideal for selling newspapers, which of course leads to espresso, without which a newspaper would be dry indeed. But what good is a newspaper and a morning drink without a table–and–chair? So soon enough there is a new hangout, an ongoing liveliness to make the parking lot more human, and an additional attraction for the store's customers.

BUILD BUS SHELTERS WITH PUBLIC SERVICES

Do any transit systems sell espresso at bus shelters? Such services are standard at larger terminals.

Of course it doesn't have to be only espresso. That's just an example. Many transit stops are too small —with too few riders—to support any services at all. But surely some goodly number of bus stops generate enough pedestrian traffic to support an espresso bar, newspaper and magazine kiosk, bank machine, flower shop, shoe-shine stand, video rental in the larger ones, or at the very least a public telephone.

Large terminals often have small shops and services—consider Grand Central Station—so why make the small stop more pleasant?

The transportation authority might build a kiosk with a "pop-out" end and entrepreneurs would "plug-in" their own self-contained gear. The authority should not do too much: utility lines (particularly a telephone line for security) would be sufficient. The authority might be paid a percentage rent to reflect truly excellent locations and to keep the whole thing honest. The successful coffee monger would inevitably gain the status of informant on bus schedules, lost dogs and cats and general watch-keeper.

SANTA CRUZ, CALIFORNIA

PIONEER SQUARE, SEATTLE

USE SOUND TO PERMIT CONVERSATION

Not only spies but ordinary folks can benefit from white noise to give them privacy. This park is located on a harsh urban corner where no one would want to spend much time chatting. Yet it provides a little bit of pastoral peace and creates privacy for conversation with white noise from a waterfall.

PROMOTE GROWING

The urge to plant and cultivate is deep but not easily satisfied if you have no ground of your own. 'P-Patches' are common ground where people can lease their own patch of dirt (typically from a city agency) and gain support from others. It is in such informal places that neighbors can meet and the practical wisdom of older people can be passed along.

UNIVERSITY DISTRICT, SEATTLE, PHOTO BY BARBARA GRAY

THE SURROGATE HOSTESS, SEATTLE

ALLOW STRANGERS TO SIT TOGETHER

Some out-of-town restaurateurs came to visit. They praised one restaurant highly and complimented the proprietor. "We love it! It's fab! The only thing you've got to change are the tables. They are too big! They're big enough for twelve!!" The proprietor smiled. Without the large tables, his restaurant wouldn't be a neighborhood hangout.

To join a stranger at a table for two or four is, for Americans, a very forward act. It is an aggressive and committing gesture, unless the seat is the last one in the house and one can point to the excuse of "necessity."

But to sit down at a common table (when there is nothing but common tables) at which a stranger is al-ready sitting, is nothing at all except playing by house rules. To make an idle remark to that stranger, to which he or she can casually respond or just as casually decline, is nothing out of the ordinary and for shy people, a more comfortable engagement.

The great abyss of urban loneliness is bridged by the large table of this restaurant; this 'third place,' and such casual contact is what cities are all about.

The only warning: such community tables are a public place, albeit small. They are not the place to propose marriage, interview for a job, or negotiate the "big deal."

Another danger: such third-place socializing becomes addictive.

CAPITOL HILL, SEATTLE

BUILD-IN BUS-STOP SEATING

This modest gesture to the street is well-used by neighbors waiting for the bus. (It was, in fact; but the photographer was shy and waited for them to board their bus before shooting.)

The landlord lost some rentable square footage but the neighborhood gained a speck of sheltered repose.

CREATE PUBLIC SPACES WITH SEATS

Seats of any kind are an invitation and an announcement: "This is a public space. Sit down and give your brain a rest." It doesn't take much. One can create a public realm by simply giving people the opportunity to sit and linger.

WALLINGFORD, SEATTLE

CAPITOL HILL, SEATTLE

QUENCH THE THIRST FOR COMMUNITY

This corner is every bit as barren and unfriendly as it appears to be. Yet the urban thirst for new experiences and stimulation is so great (and obvious to all) that even here in an urban Sahara the entrepreneur can—with the most minimal of investment—create an oasis for people to 'hang out, meet people, swap ideas'—as the stand's sidewalk board (to the right) proposes.

Like the lichen—which pioneers the barest and

CAPITOL HILL, SEATTLE

most inhospitable mountain summit and gradually through its own chemical action breaks down the hardest rock into soil where plants can grow—any refreshment is nice but the espresso bar particularly creates a fertile ground for community.

Again, government action can thwart such small improvements as this espresso bar. But its creation—so very vital to the real life of cities—is beyond institutional reach.

WALLINGFORD CENTER, SEATTLE, PHOTO BY BARBARA GRAY

USE MOVABLE CHAIRS

Communities are not announced by planners but emerge out of places which people make their own. Spaces to sit and chat allow such ownership to develop. People gain such a sense of ownership by lingering at a spot.

Enliven a sterile plaza with tables and chairs. They are inexpensive, flexible and allow the users to program the space on a short-term basis. People can rearrange them to face into or away from the sun and wind, to avoid noise, to better hear one another, to accommodate the larger group or to provide privacy for the couple or individual.

William Whyte, the observer of public space, observed that there is an inescapable ritual of sitting down. As the sitter takes a chair, she shifts it—if only a few inches—and in doing so she exerts her territoriality, making the space more her own. A space becomes more meaningful when people are allowed to create this personal and temporary territoriality with movable chairs. One might fear the hassle and loss from loose seating but the comfort level is worth the cost.

LET READERS SIP

A new and welcome trend in bookstores is to allow customers to eat and drink (once the book or magazine has been bought, of course).

"Oh! Is that the new issue of_____ ? Anything good in it?"

The magazine or book, its cover quite visible, acts like a State's sign at a political convention, bringing together those of like inclination and interest.

Bauhaus & Books, Capitol Hill, Seattle

KNOWING WHERE YOU ARE

KNOWING WHERE YOU ARE

It is very disturbing to be lost; it is a nightmare. Accurate orientation, even if unconscious, gives us a sense of comfort, safety and the territoriality we need to take action in defense of our community.

Senator Bill Bradley's genius as a basketball player, wrote John McPhee, stemmed from his peripheral vision. It gave him an extraordinary sense of *knowing where you are* on the basketball court. He could see a teammate ready to throw or an opponent ready to pounce out of the corner of his eye and beyond the range of most players. He had a split-second jump. He was always poised and comfortable because he knew what was going on around him.

So, too, for all of us on the larger court of city life. The earth is a very big place and the modern metropolis bombards us with information: roads, buildings, signs. And when they all look the same—all too often true these days—it is easy to lose orientation, to become confused, lost and isolated. Small things repeated again and again give us a sense of place and situation within the enormity of the modern city: street signs designed to be seen even at night (or in the daytime if one is partially-sighted), bulletin boards and interpretive signs, landmarks visible from many places,

A village is small enough to be comprehensible

windows onto the visible workplace. Familiarity in a city breeds comfort.

We orient ourselves by listening; and we learn by observing. But the quickest test of knowledge, and the fastest way to gain an intimate understanding, is to teach another. Such articulation forces us to wear the subject very closely. When *we* are the teacher, the guide who is orienting others, we become more at home. The *Great Gatsby*'s narrator tells us how he had come to New York to seek his fortune and had taken a bungalow in a suburban "commuting town."

> It was lonely for a day or so until one morning some man, more recently arrived than I, stopped me on the road. "How do you get to West Egg village?" he asked helplessly.
> I told him. And as I walked on I was no longer lonely. I was a guide, a pathfinder, an original settler. He had casually conferred on me the freedom of the neighborhood.

One of the most appealing things about the village—of any scale—is that it is small enough to be comprehensible. "Here is the Main Street. Here is the grocery. Here is the school." One knows without special training and education. To make a comfortable city or an urban village, leave signs and clues that tell people where they are.

PARIS, FRANCE

GIVE PEOPLE THE TIME OF DAY

Place clocks in public places. It is a simple convenience and represents the deeper social coordination given by our system of time.

There is a tyranny of time: we meter out our days for dollars, the long nightfall of 'no-time' looms over our every day, and time is a gift we give to each other when we care.

But above all in a market economy, time is a useful tool to organize our lives. Having clocks readily visible, though not as useful now in the age of cheap watches and car radios, is still a small nicety, particularly at a bus stop.

GAS WORKS PARK, SEATTLE, "SUNDIAL" BY CHUCK GREENING AND KIM LAZARE

Use Foreign Tongues

It's a gracious and courteous gesture to adjust one's language to the eyes and ears of visitors. For travelers in a distant land a little bit of their own tongue is reassuring. It is an essential for any city claiming to be international.

Tell Time by the Sun

This sun dial built into the ground (on the preceding page) reminds us that time is rooted in the natural cycles of the earth and sun. It was not invented by Swatch.® The ancients could make amazing predictions with shadows. Here, one is invited to tell the time of day by using one's own body as an indicator.

Amplify Traffic Lights

People who can't see well still need to get around. These traffic lights give them a signal they can *hear* to tell them when it's safe to cross the street. The small speakers (circled) below the light *chirp* when it's clear to walk in the north-south direction and *cuckoo* when it's "green" east-west.

GOVERNMENT LOCKS, SALMON BAY, SEATTLE

SALT LAKE CITY, UTAH

FISH LADDER OBSERVATION WINDOW, GOVERNMENT LOCKS, SALMON BAY, SEATTLE

REVEAL DESTRUCTION AND REDEMPTION

Many people grow up thinking that the natural cycle of the year starts with football and ends with baseball. It is important that from the earliest possible age people get a sense of other natural cycles, such as the upstream migration of the salmon.

Early in this century, the Corps of Engineers built a set of locks to connect the saltwater of Puget Sound to the freshwater of Lake Washington. Salmon, however, are not boats and need the stimulation of rushing water. The Locks disrupted their passage. To restore the run, the Corps built a fish ladder, an artificial switchback of swiftly running water to the side of the locks.

Here, at a window below the water's surface, a mother and child see the salmon as it migrates from saltwater to freshwater.

The irony is that without human agency, this viewpoint would not need to exist.

Enhance Neighborhood Identity with Street Trees

Repeat the same species of tree on one block, then a different species on a different block. Or perhaps different trees for longer street–lengths or even a whole neighborhood. Naturally, there are issues of monoculture and species diversity and resistance to spread of disease which arise when one wants to plant a large area with one species; but certainly a block might not be too big an area for one type.

The pattern of planting will be evident, enhance a sense of place and give veracity to neighborhood names such as *Magnolia* and *Madrona*. Flowering trees provide an unfolding progression through the seasons to tie the city together.

Burlingame, California

Entering Aurora Avenue, Seattle

Make Signs Speak Directly

We live in the midst of an ongoing public conversation; it consists of the written signs we use to give directions and explanation. A sign that merely said *Be Careful* would not be nearly as effective as this one, placed by a concerned neighboring restaurant. Traffic engineers know that in some situations, the unique and nonstandard sign catches the driver's attention and speaks more forcefully.

Identify the Crop

These days it is mainly farmers who can tell what crop is growing; it is virtually an unknown skill for the vast majority who live in the city and suburbs. So signs which tell the names of the crops are useful.

Contrary to Ms. Stein, there is always a there, *there*. But few people can see it. The delight of travel with a geographer (or other expert in landscape) is that each turn of the road and roll of the hill brings new objects onto stage for observation, identification, and discussion.

En route to Bend, Oregon

EVELENE AND GEORGE
BULLOCK

INVITE YOU TO
'SIT AND STAY'

Green Lake, Seattle

Encourage People to Leave Their Mark

They really don't need much encouragement: only an outlet. And it works out for the common good. As people grow older and more able to be philanthropic, their urge to be remembered in their old age and after their death becomes more compelling.

This urge for immortality is an ancient one; the Lascaux cave drawings are not diminished by describing them as a very brilliant piece of graffiti left behind so that the future would remember them.

No less than great museums, the Seattle parks department has recognized this very natural and human urge and capitalizes on it. It has a gift program which specifies items, locations, donations, and so on.

The couple who gave this park bench are now ever more rooted in their city's history.

埠華崙砵

PORTLAND, OREGON

CREATE GATEWAYS FOR NEIGHBORHOODS

The medieval gate around the walled city was a way to create security. In the modern city there is pressure on civic authorities to turn public streets into private ones by allowing neighbors to install real, lockable gates; such an approach signals defeat in our effort to create civility.

But the gateway as a mere announcement can also create neighborhood spirit—and security—even if it is merely a token frame. Organized police work best with people who feel ownership of their neighborhood; small symbols, like an entry arch to a neighborhood, help to create that feeling. Suburban home–builders have known this for years and often put decorative pillars and columns at the entrance to their tracts. Should not city planners also be concerned with the sense of identity in the neighborhoods?

LET PEDESTRIANS SEE FROM BRIDGES

Bridges provide a marvelous opportunity to see and comprehend the landscape without even going to any place special; bridges are *already* at a special place: where a road crosses a river or a deep ravine. Such places have historic importance; cities grew up around them because they were places where goods had to be taken off the donkey and loaded on the boat and vice versa. The control of bridges has been of great importance in both war and trade. Bridges—often difficult to build—are prizes and a focal point in any competition.

They are still very important but in the auto age they have become narrower in focus. Our single-mindedness about moving cars has led to bridges without places for cyclists or walkers, much less mere sightseers. But bridges can provide a delightful place to stop and ponder that which they cross.

VISTA DRIVE, PORTLAND, OREGON

DETAIL THE GRADE

Fairly often in the course of working with architects the issue of grades and steepness might appear. The architect might try to explain why a driveway can't be built from this side of the lot or why steps—rather than a ramp—are needed in another situation. The explanation always refers to *degrees* or *percent* of slope. One might wonder what that feels like in real-world terms. One accepts their opinion that a ramp over, say, 18 percent grade is marginal, but one might want to experience it for oneself. Where could one go to *sense* steepness? The response is always a shrug, even though a fine school of architecture is only 12 short blocks away. Certainly design students need a visceral understanding of the difference between 10 and 18 percent (or is it *degrees?*) One might expect the university neighborhood to be scattered with marks on the pavement indicating different slopes so that the students could go out and experience the difference in grades before taking the exams.

SAN FRANCISCO

JOHN BASTYR COLLEGE, WALLINGFORD, SEATTLE

IDENTIFY THE PLANTS

Naturopathic medicine is based on principles of self-healing and uses derivatives from ancient medicinal plants. On a south-facing slope next to the sidewalk a college of naturopathic medicine grows many of them to educate its students.

To the casual passerby it is a jumble of unusual plants. The key map shows which plant is where and reaches out to the neighborhood so that it, too, understands the college's approach to health.

Explain the Rule

Many of us, libertarians at heart, only reluctantly admit that in order to maintain civic order and ecological balance, there are times when it is necessary to tell people what not to do. But rules are most effective if the reason *why* is also explained. In this sign, children and parents understand why we must curtail the natural and sometimes charitable impulse to feed the animals.

Reveal the Global Framework

Latitude and longitude were one of the earliest methods by which we organized our world. But real as this measure may be, its scale is so vast as to be quite incomprehensible (blue-water sailors to the side).

An occasional reminder about where we are in this enormous global framework might be educational as well as amusing.

Green Lake, Seattle

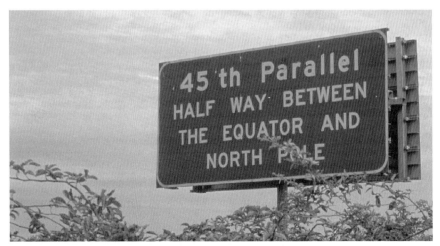

On Interstate 5, heading north, at the 45th Parallel

OLD SEAFIRST BUILDING, SEATTLE

ORIENT WITH MUSIC

Parking garages are typically confusing and disorienting. There is no outside light or view; there are no interior visual cues. All the cars and floors look the same. It is easy to forget where you are parked.

In this building the management created a musical theme—each floor a different city with characteristic music—to help people remember where they parked.

LONGVIEW, WASHINGTON

EXPLAIN SIGNAL SYNCHRONIZATION

For greater efficiency, traffic lights down the length of an avenue may often be set to turn green in sequence, so that drivers may maintain a steady and even speed. It would be helpful to drivers and more efficient overall if they were explicitly alerted to the appropriate pace. There's nothing as foolish as hiding a useful system from its target users.

It should be noted that these systems are generally hostile to creating a pedestrian-oriented neighborhood because they are designed to simply speed traffic *though* and not much more. But such traffic measures will be with us for a while so at least do them well.

BUILD BULLETIN BOARDS

An urban village will surely include bulletin boards. They are a communications medium just as surely as is a television station except that they are a two-way system. Bulletin boards are cheap neighborhood mass media, efficient for the cost, and fun.

One can measure the health and vivacity of any type of community (town, neighborhood or organization) by looking at its bulletin board. Likewise, a prospective employee can learn much by perusing a company's bulletin boards.

Some condominium associations and supermarkets do not allow bulletin boards because they are "too messy." That's a sad mistake. Communications is the heart of the word and the concept of *community*. It's a sign of organizational bleakness if there are nothing but official notices. It's a bad sign, too, when there are private notices

...measure the health and vivacity of community... by looking at its bulletin board.

but they have been retyped by the management or placed onto standard forms. Even worse are those bulletin boards enclosed within locked glass doors.

One interesting new development in bulletin boards, and a tribute to the continuing vitality of the entrepreneurial impulse, is the emergence of Posting Services. They will take your notice and place them on more bulletin boards than you might have thought even existed. One posting service guarantees posting at 120 locations for $55. As each bulletin board is managed by its owner, it's hard to predict exactly how long a notice will be posted, but typically it is two weeks to a month. Such a caretaker is a critical part of a healthy bulletin board. Someone must prune and cull the old notices and someone must tame the overly-aggressive one from bullying its smaller neighbors.

NANTUCKET, MASSACHUSETTS

IDENTIFY WATERSHEDS

After a landscape has been utterly transformed by urbanization, it's difficult to remember what was there before, what still underlies the concrete. It is always astonishing to come across a construction site in the middle of a city—especially the central business district with its towers—and see that dirt—real dirt—is still underneath the concrete. It is very easy to forget that at one time—not very long ago—the entire world was wilderness and a road was a rare blessing. (One of the benefits of wilderness travel is that it reminds us why we have chosen the path of civilization).

Likewise with watersheds: even though the stream may be long buried under streets and sidewalks, and running through culverts and storm sewers, it still exists and so does its drainage basin. These signs remind us that no matter how much concrete has been poured, earth abides.

REMIND PEOPLE WHERE THE WATER GOES

Out of sight, out of mind. That's a good explanation for why people will dump things like used motor oil down the drain when they wouldn't consider dumping it into their own swimming pool.

This stencil reminds people that the black hole of the sewer is really just an entry way to another world: our lakes, rivers and oceans. It gives a practical message, reminds them of the law and also communicates that some individual person—not distant "government"— cares about the fish.

PARIS, FRANCE

OLYMPIA, WASHINGTON

PUT MAPS ON SIDEWALKS

Any detail that helps us know where we are makes a city more comfortable.

These sidewalk maps help resident and visitor to get around without getting lost. It would be logical and obvious to put them inside every bus-shelter. In the coming digital era, we should expect interactive maps. How helpful it would be to know the best route to such-and-such an address or the location of the nearest Thai restaurant.

Leave No Black Holes of Information Where Rumor and Discord May Flourish

Woodland Park Zoo, Seattle

Paris, France

No one likes surprises, especially if the surprise may be an unpleasant one. Most people consider anything new in their neighborhood to be unpleasant. It is wise public policy that proposed development should be announced and comment from neighbors solicited. Naming the architect

and developer will add accountability. (The unwise part is that permits may sometimes be issued by the pound: one weighs the letters *for* and those *against,* and the permit is issued to the greatest weight and, mixing senses, the highest decibels.)

Developers need not look at these signs in only a negative light. Use them—within the guidelines, of course!—in order to sell the project. This sign for the Woodland Park Zoo is a sales tool, as well as public notice.

The standard *white board* from Vancouver is, by force of Pavlovian conditioning, a more forceful announcement and seems to call forth action just as the red cloth animates the raging bull. Of course, with the architect's name on it, at least people knew whom to call!

Communication *during* construction is also a good idea. People are genuinely interested in knowing what's

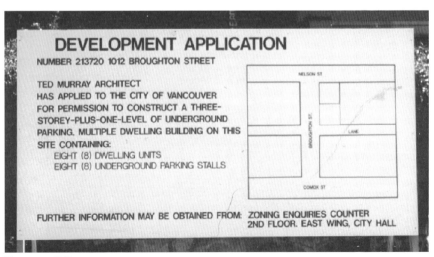

Vancouver, B.C.

going on. Sometimes they need to know whom to contact to complain and sometimes out of the sheer fascination with and vicarious joy of building. One sign comes right to the point: ("What is happening here?") and gives people an understanding of their environment and stronger sense of connection to it. Another one explains the rules on working hours. Yet another one from Paris shows that concern for the built environment is a global phenomenon.

DIVULGE BUS SCHEDULES

One of the more frustrating aspects of riding public transit is never being sure if one is early or late for the bus or even if the bus is running that day at all. I remember as a child waiting for several hours in cold weather for a bus that wasn't even in service.

Of course the truly excellent system would have buses departing so often that a schedule would be unnecessary. But in lieu of that day (unlikely to happen soon) put schedules at each stop.

Visible Workplaces

The world has become so complex that we easily lose touch with how it operates. This was not always so. In a simpler time, the commercial and industrial processes happened at a smaller and more accessible scale. One could see a national economy at work. That is rare now, which is sad because understanding the basic processes of our world helps us understand our own position in it.

One of the negative effects of urbanization and factory production is that people have little understanding that somebody, somewhere actually made the objects we see around us. Children especially should be able to see the way things are put together. The holistic viewpoint needed by the citizens of the future can be encouraged by exposing people to whole processes.

Further, there are few things more pleasing than to watch other people work, especially when the worker is skilled and the work is intriguing and involving. But few places allow close observation of other people as they shape the world.

Let the Entire Process Be Seen

This glassblowing shop allows the visitor to see the creation of a glass object from raw material to finished product.

Granville Island, Vancouver, B.C.

VESSELS AND GEAR

FISHERMEN'S TERMINAL, SALMON BAY, SEATTLE

EXPLAIN UNUSUAL EQUIPMENT

The fishing fleet moors here and repairs its nets and gear in full view. The port provides attractive signs which explain different aspects of commercial fishing. The docks themselves, too, are open to the public to walk on. At first, when the design was unveiled, the fishermen were concerned that the lack of a fence would lead to accidents. But that has not been so. A certain common sense keeps people out of the way.

CHILDREN IN THE CITY

BOSTON, MASSACHUSETTS

CHILDREN IN THE CITY

My city has the progressive policy of broadcasting its city council deliberations on the city-owned cable-TV station. One day the council was talking about children and the city.

It was a very interesting discussion about family composition and its relation to zoning rules and dwelling size. Like many American cities, my town is concerned about middle-class flight; this is understood to mean 'families' moving out of the city to the suburbs. The council was pondering what, if anything, to do about this phenomenon. Some people were arguing for urban housing that would accommodate children: *child-compatible* housing. Others wanted to put more of an emphasis on revitalizing the school system.

I thought their concern about families with children leaving Seattle to be quite fascinating and intelligent. But I had a moment of concern—a moment of black humor—that others might misinterpret the council and see them at the top of a slippery-slope: a politically-correct city council discussing family composition! Might someone fear a notion—lurking in deep background—that along with numerical goals for such things as water quality, job growth, and traffic congestion there might also be a goal for the number of children in the city? For once you have decided that the city should be a place for children, wouldn't one obvious way to ensure that your policies are working be to urge people to have children? But the council never even got close to such foolishness.

Their question was not whether or not children live in the city *per se.* The council was concerned that the city is a hospitable environment for children. Children are like the canaries in the coal mine: an indicator species of urban health. Children are small and vulnerable and need to be protected. If a city lacks children, then it is because parents have assessed the environment and have decided, one family after another over the privacy of the dining room table, to remove to a safer place. But where parents won't raise children, we might all hesitate to live, for such a place presents an environment uncomfortable, noisy, and dangerous.

Children are like the canaries in the coal mine: an indicator species of urban health.

PLACE PLAYGROUNDS IN SHOPPING DISTRICTS

Combine adult seating with playgrounds in business districts. These places may be small. Place them at easily accessible locations, and especially in shopping districts. This one is carved out of the public right–of–way on the edge of a busy street. (It serves to narrow and neck down the street to slow traffic as well.)

Children are more open about striking up acquaintances than are adults. So like puppies, children ease the way and make it natural and easy for adults to say hello.

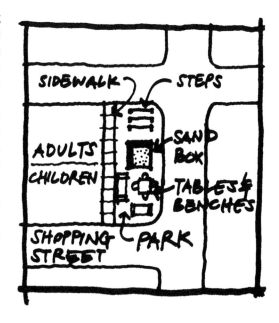

GREEN LAKE, SEATTLE

BUILD-IN BABY-SITTING

Children are more at ease when they have something to do. Most critically, children bother adults less when they feel at ease. Let them draw on walls which are primed for their touch as they sit at chairs designed for their size.

BUILD TO CHILD SCALE

Building spaces that are sized for children is a courtesy.

GRANVILLE ISLAND, VANCOUVER, B.C.

ANY ONE OF SEVERAL THOUSAND McDONALD'S®

PROVIDE PLAYGROUNDS AT RESTAURANTS

Mothers say that the places where a parent can lunch with friends while the children play safely are rare. It is a sad commentary on the state of city life—and a tribute to the acumen of McDonald's®—that it is one of the few private institutions which provide such a comfort.

Parents and children need to be together but without stumbling over and interfering with each other.

PROVIDE PLAYGROUNDS IN UNLIKELY PLACES

Children do not have the patience of adults; perhaps it's even their definition. Traveling with children can sometimes be trying because they get bored so easily. So provide little playgrounds even in the midst of intense development. Shown here is a playground in a bus/ferry terminal where tired parents can let their children catch up.

Let Infants (and Parents!) Travel in Style

Diapers have to be changed when they have to be changed, and not at the convenience of adults. So make it easy for parents with children to travel by providing appropriate counters in public restrooms.

Society has a stake in having happy homes. Part of happiness is travel. Why should parents have to give up sightseeing when there are little ones? No reason at all if we make accommodation for parents.

People with disabilities are now to be considered in the design of buildings. Perhaps public accommodation should consider children as well.

Sign on door, Lonsdale Quay, Vancouver, B.C.

Lonsdale Quay, Vancouver, B.C.

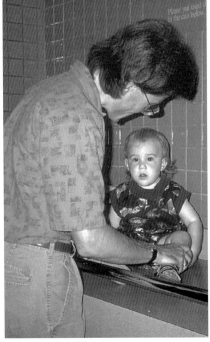

Woodland Park Zoo, Seattle

FEELING SAFE

FEELING SAFE

Human communications flourishes only in safety. A prerequisite for meeting people or getting to know them better is feeling safe, secure and unthreatened.

Safety is at the root of all city politics. Humans initially came together in settlements for increased security from wild animals, flood, famine, and enemies. When the chips are down, we flee to people for safety. There is safety in numbers.

Of course very large cities with great numbers and high levels of anonymity have had crime problems for thousands of years. But now, greater mobility gives us the choice to add distance to our protective mechanisms: to move to ever more dispersed suburbs because cities make us uneasy—except in our locked cars. (And even cars are not safe-haven, as car-jacking shows.) So part of the question of city design— and suburb design, for that matter— must be "what patterns allow us to feel safe?" Without trying to explain the causes of crime, can design contribute to safety?

The first principle of security in any situation is surveillance. *The* basic technique of urban security is natural surveillance and human presence ; and this should be no surprise. 'Intelligence' is the first need for the army at war and the pedestrian on the street. Consider the function of the night-watchman or the surveillance camera: deter wrong-doers simply because they know they will be observed and observation precedes arrest. But surveillance in our context does not mean formal watching but the casual observation that comes naturally, for example, when one is sitting on the porch after dinner.

The basic technique of urban security is natural surveillance.

The second principle is territoriality: people must view the public space as their own and thus take some responsibility for it. They must not only be able to see trouble as it develops, but they must also be willing to act and to intervene—if only to telephone the police.

The second is territoriality: people must view the public space as their own.

What these principles mean in architecture is the creation of spaces where people are present and can observe each other in a form of mutual protection *and* where they have enough sense of ownership of the street that they will intervene in some way when trouble appears.

Jane Jacobs spoke of "eyes on the street," the *presence of other human beings who care.* Not complicated but easier said than done.

WALLINGFORD, SEATTLE

OPEN THE STOREFRONT TO THE STREET

How do you make the street an interesting place where people will come to linger? Every shopping-center owner knows that you have to slow down their pace and let them be drawn in by the merchandise. The same rule applies to the street.

People are a cautious lot. We enter through the door of a strange store with some element of timidity under the watchful eye of a strange shopkeeper. So the wise merchant will make such an entrance as easy and inviting as possible. The shop with a fully opened and permeable front allows a delicate, slow and uncommitted entrance. You stop to look at the plants on the street, then your eye is caught by an item farther back. "What's that old thing there?" And soon, without a decision, you're inside the shop. The permeable storefront is inviting and thus good merchandising.

FULLY OPEN WINDOWS

As clear as glass may be, it divides vendor from shopper. To bring the shopper into one's store, an unhindered opening creates an immediacy and intimacy as well as a shopkeeper constantly and naturally observing the street.

PIKE PLACE MARKET, SEATTLE, PHOTO BY BARBARA GRAY

PUT COPS ON BIKES

Silent, fast, and physically fit from hours of riding each day, the cop on a bike is a formidable opponent for the scoundrel. Such an officer is also accessible and puts a friendlier face on authority, which is important, as the police are few and rely on information from the general population. The police are only the tip of our security system and, like the fish, rely on the water they swim through for support.

SCATTER POLICE

'The cops are never around when you need them.' So goes the old saw. One solution is to scatter small police stations, sized for one or two officers, about the city. If a vendor sold espresso nearby—a natural gathering and gossiping spot—so much the better!

UNIVERSITY DISTRICT, SEATTLE

POLICE STATION, TOKYO, PHOTO BY CATHY TUTTLE

RESTON, VIRGINIA

ENGAGE WALKERS WITH INTERESTING SHOPFRONTS

Interesting sidewalks are busy. Busy sidewalks are safer.

There is a stretch of beach front on the island of Maui which could be one of the great promenades of the world: Kihei. It stretches for five or six miles along a grand bay. A two–lane road runs along its entire length. Much of the beach is public park. The land upland from the road is devoted to business. Between the glorious weather and the vigor of a long stroll, this indeed could be a memorable walk, the kind of stroll which by itself could draw one from a distant continent: a safe, dry, warm and interesting walk, with many shops and stores to browse and amuse and to keep the street alive and safe.

Alas. The many shops and stores are built to the strip–mall model, with the parking lot between the street and the stores. The walk along the road is boring, with no shop windows to peer into and only the hoods of the slumbering automobiles to look at. We could see some mildly interesting shops across the parking lots and wondered what they sold. But we did not go to look. Crossing the barren plain of parking lot asphalt had no appeal, in fact was positively repelling, and so we demurred; and the merchants lost sales. The parking lot was a barrier to profit.

Get close to the customer: build to the sidewalk and create interesting storefronts to give people something to look at it as they walk.

FIFTH AVENUE, SEATTLE

ALLOW STREET VENDORS

Progressive cities have a liberal policy of allowing street vendors to locate where they wish, subject to only the veto of the adjacent merchant and property owner. In Seattle, the espresso bar has filled this niche to a degree unknown in any other American (or European, for that matter) city. The result is a node of activity. One espresso entrepreneur recognized a space under a marquee, an empty niche. With espresso cart, tables and chairs, it is now a place to relax from shopping. It promotes human contact by providing a quiet eddy to schmooze out of the rushing torrent of downtown commerce.

More eyes on the street also create a real and perceived sense of safety.

KENTLANDS, MARYLAND

COULD YOU "KEEP AN EYE ON THINGS?"

Again: a principle of such simplicity that it took Jane Jacobs' enormous insight to see it. But it is an insight which applies to residential areas as much as shopping districts: eyes on the street promotes safety. The price of liberty is continual surveillance. The old rule of the sea—"one hand for yourself, one hand for the ship"—applies on shore: "One eye for yourself. One eye for the neighborhood."

Place the entrance to a residence so that the visitor knows where to enter and so that neighbors can see what's going on. The Block Watch program of many neighborhoods is a way we formalize a practice that used to be a natural part of neighborhood life when neighbors actually knew each other.

Eyes on the street provides security. Thugs know this, and as you may notice, avoid breaking into homes while neighbors watch. But hide the door and you give them an opportunity for crime. It is the continual and casual surveillance of the street *outside* by the people *inside* that provides security.

WASHINGTON, D.C.

MAKE THE MAIN ENTRANCE VISIBLE

It's an aid to security if neighbors can see the front door. Well it may not apply to this house as much as to most since the folks who live here have full time *eyes on the street* at every possible turn. But the principle is the same. The official police can't do everything and they can't do much at all without good information. So the eyes and ears of the rest of us are essential to deter crime.

Further, it's perplexing and annoying to desire to enter a building and not know where to go. It means extra walking and backtracking and, if at night or in a less-frequented area, it creates feelings of insecurity. It's a rude way to treat a guest. There is enough natural perplexity in the world. We don't need architects to give us ambiguous clues that lead us hither and yon before we can find an open door.

So make the front door obvious and start signalling its location at the sidewalk.

LITTLE NECESSITIES

A myriad of small elements adds comfort to the city and makes it...well...comfortable. They are not large and glamourous but they make a difference indeed.

Much of our public discussion attends to abstract issues such as *housing units per acre* or *levels of service* (at intersections) but it is the tiny details that create an urban village.

Stanley Park, Vancouver, B.C.

SHELTER THE TELEPHONE

The cellular telephone may have lessened the demand for public payphones. But that doesn't mean you shouldn't shelter this little outpost on the information superhighway. Many phone booths are both inconvenient and uncomfortable to use because of exposure to noise and weather.

Public phones are a safety measure for the motorist stranded at night or the child lost during the day. Don't be stingy with phones (and make 9-1-1 calls free!)

"Have a Drink on Us"

Nowadays, most of us take water for granted. But early human settlements grew up around rare wells and springs. Providing safe and cheap water through municipal waterworks was a massive social advance. In poor societies without in-home plumbing, the community well is still part of daily life.

Truly comfortable water fountains would welcome people in wheelchairs with a cantilevered drinking spout and children with steps.

CANNON BEACH, OREGON

Public Toilets are a Comfort

Public toilets are known as *comfort stations* for good reason. Even though everyone uses toilets, it's remarkable how few there are when needed—particularly clean ones. Public toilets are one of the first priorities for a comfortable city.

On a visit to New York my lunch companion announced that it was time to visit the loo. I made no motion and she reminded me that I was in the big city: "The experienced traveler should never pass-up a clean bathroom." City comfort is made of small things.

The public toilet shown here is in Europe, where there are over four thousand scattered about the public streets. It locks and cleans itself after every use. It can cost the local municipality nothing if—as is being done in San Francisco—advertising is allowed on kiosks or other street furniture.

Somewhere in Europe, photo by JC DECAUX

CANNON BEACH, OREGON

HOUSE THE GARBAGE CAN

Garbage cans are crucial to cleaner streets as they remind people simply by their quiet, patient waiting that the place for garbage is in the can and not on the sidewalk.

We should honor them by giving them a place to live, particularly in locations where there are street vendors selling food.

KEEP YOUR HEAD DRY

Awnings are a friendly gesture; they extend a building's protection to the guest who passes along the sidewalk before it. Because awnings offer such hospitality, they draw pedestrian traffic to them and benefit the business of adjacent merchants.

Buckminster Fuller said that civilization in its technology and tools is simply a way of modulating and tuning—in and out—the elements—earth, air, fire, and water. Awnings are a humble but effective way to tune out a wet head.

PIKE PLACE MARKET, SEATTLE

SEATTLE

KEEP YOUR FEET DRY

Create a narrow strip—sixteen inches or so—of concrete, brick or any hard surface at the curb and extending into the planting strip to allow a person getting out of the car to keep the feet dry.

One might think that such an insignificant detail as dry feet is too trivial to consider. But it is precisely such small details and courtesies that enrich life and make some cities a pleasure. Without such details, urban planning is simply the board game *Monopoly*® but for adults.

Make It Easy for Pets to be Polite

There is general agreement that pets are good for the mental health of their owners. This is so, particularly in atomized urban areas where many people lack companions. Like babies, but even more so, pets are a vivid way for people to identify themselves and to recognize kindred spirits. Dogs are also an aid to safety by giving warning of prowlers.

But dogs, to some degree, create a problem. So...

...IF YOU HAVE THESE FRIENDS,

PARIS, FRANCE

AND YOU HAVE THESE RULES...

Please leash and
**clean up
after your
dog**

IT'S THE LAW
MAX. FINE $ 500 .
PARKS BYLAW #9 (C)

VANCOUVER, B.C.

NOT FOR LITTER

DOG-WASTE ONLY

LONDON

...THEN GET SOME OF THESE TOOLS.

North Vancouver, B.C.

CELEBRATE THE STATION

Gas stations (or electric vehicle re-charge stations) will be with us for some time. Let even the very mundane be pleasing:

I pulled over to take this picture.
My companion said 'What's *that*?'
'A gas station.'
'Really??!!' he replied.
Case closed.

PROVIDE ASH TRAYS

A nasty habit indeed but it's even nastier when the only place to extinguish the smoldering butt is on the sidewalk or between your thumb and forefinger. Yes, the public ash tray does raise the issue of benign tolerance for others' weaknesses vs. encouragement of vice, but at least it dampens the problem of litter.

GOVERNMENT LOCKS, SEATTLE

SMOOTHING EDGES:

BUFFERS AND SHIELDS

SMOOTHING EDGES:
BUFFERS AND SHIELDS

Sharp edges shock. Shock can be dangerous. Shock can kill.

To paraphrase Lord Acton: 'Change shocks. Dramatic change shocks dramatically.' Sharp transitions in the built landscape are no exception.

Nature abhors a sharp transition or a rough edge. The forces of gravity, and of wind and water tend over any period of time to smooth out sudden, jarring geological boundaries, to create gradual transitions. We avoid rough edges in social conduct, too, with gracious talk and diplomacy. And we do the same with our built landscape.

We build walls for privacy from other people's curiosity. We grow hedges to shield us from the view of the junk-yard. We build roofs to keep us dry and houses with operable windows or air-conditioning to keep the heat away. We create buffers so that we can tune-in some things and tune-out others.

Robert Frost may have spoken ironically: "Good fences makes good neighbors." But indeed the defined boundary is an aid to neighborliness, if only because we know where responsibilities end and begin.

City zoning codes create boundaries to separate uses which are incompatible. Of course, by carrying this separation so far, we create the need for cars for even the simplest trips, and hence once again need buffers. For example, consider the typical convenience store. When it is built next to residences—and where else would it be?—the parking lot needs buffering to be a good neighbor. But the buffering is needed not because of the retail use *per se* but because of its accessory parking lot.

In cities we need buffers from blank walls and from automobiles—both in motion or parked. It is particularly our precious cars which we seek to keep at bay. The car is our central nonhuman relationship and urban design challenge. The purpose of urban buffers is to smooth the edge between the place of cars and the places of people.

What an irony. How perverse. Our most valued places are often sites which lack our most valued possession: cars. We have roadless areas in the wilderness, we seek to build *pedestrian-friendly* areas to which we can drive and then walk around. No one is immune. Our *own* car is a gem and the freedom it grants is a pleasure. But we love to be in a place without being bothered by *other people's* cars.

But many of our buffers

> **O**ur most valued places are often sites which lack our most valued possession: cars.

to avoid the blank wall and visual monotony. Large scale uses often meet the street with a blank wall because their transition to the street is not considered important by their large and single-minded institutional owners.

But *blankness* seems to be an innate human horror. Shelley speaks of Ozymandias' stare as "blank and pitiless as the sun." One common human nightmare is to be chased by faceless beings. Turning one's face away from another is a put–down.

Lewis Mumford explains *his* generation's rapid adoption of the barren Modern Style as an overreaction to his parents' generation's horror of the blank wall and their consequent fascination with things. In his autobiography *Sketches from Life* he says:

"Blankness" seems to be an innate human horror.

The clutter of interior decoration in middle-class homes at this period is almost indescribable. The most contemptuous word that could be applied to an interior in those days was 'bare'—'as bare as a barn.' I still remember that in one of Conan Doyle's early novels the young heroine was almost driven to insanity when her cruel calculating guardian confined her to a bare, white-washed room. The bareness did it!

We decorate to buffer ourselves from blankness...from madness.

Soften Walls

One very common edge is presented by the retaining wall which is a necessity when lots are small and there are slopes. Some way must be found to create a transition between two elevations.

Often it is concrete, blank and forbidding. In certain situations it can be softened. The one to the right is made of interlocking pieces of precast concrete with soil placed in between. Plants grow there and water can flow through to relieve pressure build up from behind the wall.

North Vancouver, B.C.

SEATTLE ART MUSEUM

SCREEN THE PARKING LOT WITH DISPLAY CASES

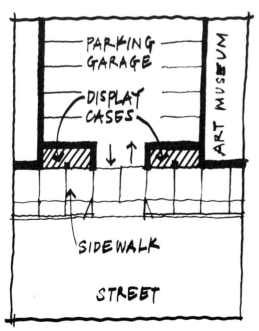

Few things are less comfortable than the blank wall. They are boring to walk by and make no contribution to safety—no human surveillance. But sometimes they are unavoidable.

These display cases were allowed by the building officials as a substitute for retail spaces. Though a weak echo for the intent of the zoning code—visual interest, security through eyes on the street, and so on—they do effectively screen the surface parking lot from the sidewalk. They give passersby something to look at and advertise the activities of the museum of which they are a part.

HEDGE-IN THE ENTRANCE

In residential areas, too, the relationship of the house to the sidewalk is important.

Walking on the sidewalk before the gaping maw of a 2-car garage and attendant curb-cut is not a pleasant or urbane experience, particularly when there are several double garages in a row. In cities with few alleys it is a common experience. There is no other way for a car to enter the site except across the front sidewalk and front yard.

This house solves the problem by necking down the entry with a hedge, paving the forecourt with bricks and softening the roof-edge with wisteria.

In a neighborhood with few muggers this is a very civilized solution. It probably violates the zoning code requirements for sight triangles (how much you can see) at driveways, but it *works.*

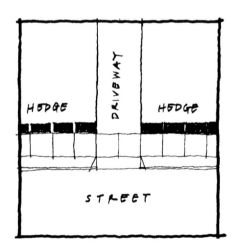

SHIELD WITH ELEVATION

Many military tactics involve working with earthforms to take advantage of the enemy. One takes the high ground above the enemy to defend and one slips through the depressed swale to outflank. Shielding the car from view is similar to defending against any adversary.

One parking lot was set *lower* than the level of an adjacent sidewalk; one looks over the cars. The other lot is set *above* an adjacent road so that one cannot even see the cars. (So hidden is the parking lot that when I first reviewed this photo, I could not remember what it was supposed to show!

WALLINGFORD, SEATTLE

REDMOND, WASHINGTON

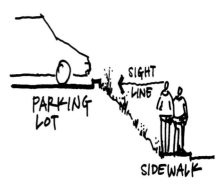

ST. HELENA, CALIFORNIA

NARROW THE PARKING LOT ENTRANCE

Neck down the entrance to create a landscaped area. It is an easy way to civilize a parking lot where it meets the sidewalk. This one is a little the worse for wear but imagine the desolation if these trees were gone.

Again, it is these small and modest improvements to the city's physical shape, repeated over and over again, which give a city its vitality and interest and comfort.

Unfortunately, these small items of civic courtesy do not show up in the glossy architectural and design magazines, but they are in fact the truly important items.

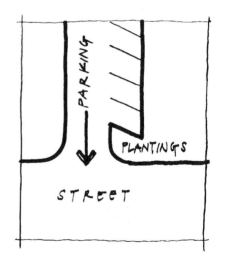

Longview, Washington

PLANT STREET TREES FOR PREMIUM VALUE

Even streets of modest houses gain a grandeur and presence when treed. Old money need not be the only ones to have old trees.

If time is money, then these street trees are very expensive. Yet a 4" caliper tree can be planted for merely $300, including maintenance for the first five year's life, when it is most vulnerable. The expensive part is time: foresight and patience. Cities would do well to spend less energy on contentious greenbelt regulation and more on planting trees on their existing 'barrens'—their rights-of-way.

Gain the economies of scale by letting landscape contractors bid block-by-block: not a tree here and tree there but blocks, indeed neighborhoods, of varying trees. The homeowner could choose to have a tree set in its curb-side planting-strip by checking a box on the utility bill, with payments stretched out over some reasonable time.

On an economic basis, street tree planting will more than pay for itself in increased property values, particularly when done on a neighborhood-wide basis. One tree in front of one house is fine but the real impact is when an entire district is treed.

Planting 150,000 trees on the public right-of-way of a medium-sized city might cost each homeowner $60 a-year for 5 years. But the trees would likely boost the value of each home by at least $1,000 to $5,000 at the end of that 5 year period. Three hundred dollars invested and one thousand dollars returned! That's a fair return.

Maintain the Parking Lot Landscape

It takes no high sensibility to critique the strip-mall. But as nasty as those auto-oriented suburban strips may be, they will be with us for a while. So imagine them with really lush landscaping. Most lots are large enough to accommodate quite a few shrubs and trees; and landscaping is fairly inexpensive. Such a small thing and so much impact.

Imagine if most parking lots were surrounded by green! We might still have auto-oriented strip-malled neighborhoods. But what an improvement! So let's pass a law...we think. But the key is ongoing maintenance which is beyond the reach of regulation.

Many cities have rules that require landscaping in new construction; some require irrigation systems or the planting of drought-tolerant species. Others even require some nebulous language about continued maintenance. But the key to pleasant landscaping is in the hands of the property-owner. What turns the key is the shared social expectation—not the hammer of the law—that taking care of one's property is the decent thing to do. One sees this most clearly in single–family neighborhoods, where subtle but real social sanctions are brought to bear on home-owners who let their lawns go unmowed. But such social expectations also command respect in commercial districts and will motivate the property-owner to go beyond mere purchase of plants and actually maintain them.

The larger lesson of this parking lot is to do small things to make life more comfortable *now*.

CARMEL, CALIFORNIA

SAVE EVEN ONE TREE

We so love efficiency that it is surprising when we see a walkway or a road rerouted to save a tree. The trees shown here were poorly located in the first place. They had overgrown their place, were buckling the sidewalk, were "out-of-scale" or "in the way." Be gone you misplaced tree!

But someone cared and molded the right-of-way around them.

The benefits are several and varied:

• a fine old tree is saved;

• traffic must slow to negotiate the obstruction;

• people are reminded by its eccentricity that the city need not be managed as a machine for some supposed "efficiency."

The lone tree is particularly striking and a reminder that steering wheels are designed for avoiding obstacles.

PORTLAND, OREGON

PORTLAND, OREGON

TRELLIS BLANK WALLS

Blank walls have no personality. They are devoid of human attention. But sometimes they are inevitable. There are ways to make them less offensive, which in this case is by obscuring them with a trellis.

SOFTEN WITH GREEN

Money, that is. The transition from house to car is important, common and most often harsh. Soften it with decorative paving, which admittedly, is very costly. But the choice for a builder, of all but the most modest houses, is *where* to put the discretionary money. For a charming place, better cobbles on the ground than tiles on the roof. But patterned concrete—not all that more expensive than asphalt—can also do wonders.

NANTUCKET, MASSACHUSETTS

DENNY REGRADE, SEATTLE

GREEN LAKE, SEATTLE

BUILD A GRASSY BERM

We have an approach/avoidance relationship with parking lots. We need them for our personal convenience but we prefer to hide them.

This berm separates the parking lot from the sidewalk.

MAKE FENCES LOW ENOUGH TO SEE OVER

This bamboo fence creates a boundary for the realm of the automobile. Before its installation, in life's inexorable and harsh struggle to park as close as possible to the destination, drivers would park their cars across the sidewalk. This fence stops such parking and returns the sidewalk to the person on foot. But it is low and open enough that it doesn't create a security problem.

Noise Control

One of the most annoying elements of city life is noise—other people's, that is. In fact the difference between *noise* and *sound* is that you make sound—other people make noise. This is nothing new. The bane of urban life has long been noise. The diarist Pepys spoke of 17th century London's unpleasant noise. A very effective torture which leaves no visible scars is to subject a person to enormous and continuing noise.

There are three ways to deal with noise:

• *Change* its nature at the source. For example, tire producers and road designers could make low noise one of their design goals. Or active noise cancellation could actually produce counter-noise to wipe out the objectionable noise;

• *Mask* it with a more pleasant sound of your choosing; or

• *Block* it with a solid physical structure.

Use Glass to Block Noise

This wall blocks noise from a very busy arterial and yet permits a sense of the world beyond to the residents behind it.

Use White Noise from a Waterfall

The white noise of this waterfall masks street noise and makes a park usable.

False Creek, Vancouver, B.C.

WESTLAKE MALL, SEATTLE, PHOTO BY BARBARA GRAY

RAISE PROPERTY VALUES WITH WALLS

The edge of the freeway is one of the most inhospitable places in the world because of noise. This insatiable roar is part of modern urban lives and is an overall blight. It hinders conversation, is bad for mental health and dampens real property values. The freeway spreads its oppressive, dull and ever–present Niagara roar far away from Lake Ontario to every city on the grid.

One way to lessen the roar is with this freeway wall. It is an expensive piece of concrete. But its cost will in the long-run be easily recaptured from increased taxes because the neighborhoods beyond the wall will become quieter, more pleasant places to live and hence more valuable.

INTERSTATE 5 NEAR OLYMPIA, WASHINGTON

FITTING IN

DELIGHTFUL NEWBURY STREET IN BOSTON...MADE OF BUILDINGS WHOSE BUILDING ENVELOPE COULD BE
DESCRIBED ON THE BACK OF A POSTCARD...A SMALL POSTCARD AT THAT.

FITTING IN

Economic growth depends on a continuous reconstruction of society. Such rebuilding raises again and again the issue of ensuring that the new buildings do not war on the old, and thus, in the political sense, that new construction is politically sustainable.

With buildings as with humans, there is a delicate line between attracting too much attention by overly dramatic self-presentation, and being a wallflower, ignored and unnoticed. The current thought is that it is best for a new building to fit-in with the existing architectural context of its neighbors. The new building should in some way echo and mimic the materials, height, details, and behavioral patterns of its neighbors. This does not mean that the new building must exactly copy the old one but simply that it should learn from and respond to the buildings that surround it. We call this approach contextualism and while it is *au courant* and thus, to my mind, immediately suspect, it does in fact make a lot of sense. But the key to having a landscape where a new building fits-in is clear communication to the builder, and before that, fine understanding about what is most important about any particular landscape.

Architects often say that a building does or does not *talk* to its neighbors. What they describe is how a building makes reference in its own shape and material to the shapes and materials of its neighbors. A lively conversation between buildings means that the buildings relate to each other. The color of one may be picked up and amplified by another or the roofline of another may be mimicked by yet a fourth. A group of musicians will do something similar in their playing. A horn may start with a cluster of notes and the pattern will be repeated with variations by the other instruments.

Buildings are much like their human users. *Conversation* between buildings, as among humans, is a poignant sign of neighborliness. It is the height of rudeness—though all too often the expected norm in cities—for neighbors to speak not a word to each other for years on end. Buildings which do not *talk* to their neighbors are also rude.

> **Conversation between buildings, as among humans, is a poignant sign of neighborliness.**

Successful contextual development also depends on a clear conversation between the government and builders. A zoning code that speaks clearly is a practical prerequisite to fitting-in, because it is through the zoning code that the developer learns what is allowed and expected. And it is through the zoning code that society at large speaks to the individual who wishes to build. Just as a great client stands behind a great architect, a great zoning code stands behind them both.

This great zoning code will be based on a close understanding of the environment which it seeks to protect. It will, in many instances, call for *unified diversity*. Not an oxymoron, this is an approach which allows variations but only tight ones from a clear theme. For example, the great townhouse neighborhoods of Manhattan and much of Paris and Boston as shown on an earlier page are built to a very simple zoning code. The building can only be so tall; it can or must be built to the sidewalk; its entrance must be only in such a location; it must have so many windows, and so on.

One could write the zoning code for such areas on a postcard. It is a short zoning code and severe. But out of these limits grow hospitable, attractive neighborhoods. The builder must pour his creativity into narrow confines: the detailing of windows, the color of the siding, the arrangement of the entry, etc. Like any other tight and limiting form—the haiku, the sonnet, the fugue, the airplane, the rowboat—the creative and personalizing impulse must focus on only a limited set of variables.

The number of variables to be considered will depend on the tightness of the context and the degree of political desire that such context be preserved. For example, the island of Nantucket has design guidelines for its entirety, with even more specific parameters in the historic town of Nantucket. There are rules for all aspects of the building and its site; and many decisions are foreclosed. For example, flat roofs are simply not allowed. Roof pitch must be at least 4/12, or considerably steeper if neighboring structures have already set such a pattern. But Nantucket is unusual. It has both a strong architectural context and the political will to preserve it.

In general, there are a number of aspects of a building which will determine whether a building fits in or does not. For example:
- Site plan and orientation;
- Size, proportion and scale;

These are generally dictates of the local land use code and there may not be much choice for the developer.

However, there are other factors such as shape, roof line, windows and doors, exterior architectural elements, surface materials, trim and architectural details, and color.

Some codes are very restrictive and provide few choices; others are wide open and provide no sense of what

> **The only proviso with the fitting–in approach—and it is a major one— is that the existing context must be worth emulating.**

is appropriate conversation.

In codes such as Nantucket's with tight constraints—like dress codes at a parochial school—the result tends to be (or at least should be!) easy and predictable public administration. In neighborhoods governed by codes applying unified diversity, new buildings fit-in with neighbors without being slavishly identical, and may yet reflect the idiosyncrasies and preferences of owner and designer.

The only proviso with the fitting–in approach—*and it is a major one*— is that the existing context must be worth emulating, which is not often the case. Sometimes the neighborhood is in transition, such as when the zoning has been recently changed; or perhaps the existing built environment is lacking charm. In either case there is little context worth saving or emulating. Here of course the contextual approach falls apart and the developer and neighborhood are free to face the enormous challenge of creating a new context.

But in general, the contextual approach provides a just challenge for the cutting–edge school of architecture which seeks the novel for its own sake, and for the sake of career advancement.

Look Next Door for Context

The building on the left was brand-new in 1993 and made of modern materials: factory-made windows and an ersatz version of stucco. It fits in well because it follows the basic rules for commercial buildings: it is built right up to the sidewalk, it has retail on the ground-floor, the retail has windows which face the sidewalk and the main doors of the building face the street.

Of course, this building (to the left) was 'lucky' because it had a strong and straightforward neighbor to guide it.

FREMONT, SEATTLE

PARIS, FRANCE

RESPOND TO MODERN PREFERENCES AND FIT IN

Contextualism cannot reverse or deny the preferences of consumers. Modern users of both commercial and residential space have certain demands and their needs must be met or there is no sale. But it is possible to have a new building meet these demands. People like and have become accustomed to light–filled rooms. The light-colored building in the center of this photo responds to this modern demand and yet fits in with its older neighbors.

Close observation reveals that there is a new building here, which fits-

> ## Contextualism cannot reverse or deny the preferences of consumers.

in reasonably well. Certainly the new building is cleaner than the old ones and stands out for that reason. But compare the proportion of window–to–wall in the new building versus the old ones. The new building is built with modern techniques and modern materials and is able to be structurally stable with less wall and more window.; yet it *learns* from its neighbors and *responds* to them. It clearly defines the sidewalk–level pedestrian space from the floors above; there is a cornice line for the penthouses; the windows are well-defined and have texture.

BEAVERTON, OREGON

PLANT YOUR BUILDING SO IT LOOKS LIKE A HILL

Neighbors often complain with great justice that a building has "excessive height, bulk and scale." Sometimes these words are a magical talisman of archibabble which drips a gloss of academic respectability on the *not-in-my-backyard* impulse. But many times, they are correct. The real culprit is a zoning code which does not require any transition. For the builder in a site where the zoning code has erred, try to hide the excessive height, bulk and scale.

Nobody minds living in the shadow of a hill. A hill can be much bigger than any apartment building ever proposed but no one comments on its size. So plant your building, for example, so it resembles a hill. Stepping down a building helps it more closely resembles a natural form.

THE IRONICALLY NAMED "DESIGN CENTER," LOS ANGELES, CALIFORNIA

QUEEN ANNE HILL, SEATTLE

USE A SIMILAR ROOFLINE

Fitting-in the old and the new can be as simple as similar rooflines,

There are few uses whose activities are less compatible with a quiet residential street than a fire station yet whose presence is more critical to its safety.

This station was originally built in the 1950s. Fire fighting rigs have grown longer and taller since then. The fire fighters needed to remodel their station to accommodate the newer gear. It would have been very easy for an expanded fire station to

It would have been very easy for an expanded fire station to be totally incompatible.

be totally incompatible. But the designer linked the remodeled station to its single-family neighbors by size, setback from the sidewalk and roof line. The roof of the old station was popped-up and a new facade added.

The surface treatment of the fire station looks somewhat industrial and differs from its neighbors. But the consistent scale, roof line and set back allows it to fit in and to be— perhaps even because of its uniqueness—a visual asset to the neighbors.

Vancouver, B.C.

MIMIC THE OLDER BUILDING'S DETAILS

The parking garage on the left side of the photo is from the late 1980s. It works because it mimics its charming older neighbor. The window openings are of the same proportion and line up with each other across the two buildings. The facades appear to be of the same material; and the striation of the stonework in the older building is repeated in the new one, as is the cornice line. The garage also has openings at street level to match the older building, even though one only sees out while parking the car, though that is a small delight.

You could pass by and not recognize it as a garage.

The new parking garage does not 'read'— as architects say— as a parking garage but simply as a kindred addition to an older building. You could pass by and not recognize it as a garage.

From the inside as well it is a pleasure, as the big windows nicely frame the buildings across the street.

CAPITOL HILL, SEATTLE

USE SIMILAR MATERIALS

These elegant townhouses sold for $600,000 to $800,000 unfinished in the late 1980s. To one side they are bordered by even more imposing houses and to the other, far more modest structures. But on all sides, brick was common. The new townhouses' brick facades linked them with their neighbors.

ALLOW THE CORNER GROCERY

The modern convenience store is nothing new. It is traditional to forget something and need to 'run down to the store.' There is nothing new about such use; what is destructive is that our neighborhoods are often built so that the only way to reach the store is by car.

VENICE, CALIFORNIA

LOOK SMALLER FROM THE SIDEWALK

This supermarket appears significantly smaller than its over 30,000 square feet would suggest because much of its mass is set below the street grade. Its front wall at the sidewalk is only one-story high. Furthermore, because it comes right to the sidewalk, it has a traditional and reassuring air.

WESTERN AVENUE, SEATTLE

CAMOUFLAGE THE PARKING GARAGE

This site is within a block of a deep saltwater bay. It is built on fill and because of the high water table, it was not feasible to place the parking garage underground. (There would have been a constant battle with seepage into the garage due to the hydrostatic pressure on the foundation).

Thus, the parking had to be placed above grade. Rather than give up valu-able—for economics and urban design— retail space at sidewalk level, the parking garage was placed above the first floor. By bringing down the window pattern from the offices above, the architect created the appearance of a unified whole. One can be generally aware of this building for years before realizing that its first few stories above the street are a parking garage.

PARIS, FRANCE

MAKE RULES BUT ALLOW THEM TO BE BROKEN

A central premise of this book is that a comfortable city's environment is by no means random, subjective and chaotic, but is composed of many recurring patterns which are, with few exceptions, preferred by all people.

Nonetheless, a healthy city will provide room for new and unexpected design, particularly in visual appearance. All buildings need not mimic exactly their neighbors so long as in some significant way they are complementary. Harmony can be made with dissonant chords. Novelty and surprise are the spice of the city. Let

...understand what rules are being broken, and why...

there be exceptions to the rule. A variety of sites, circumstances and tastes dictate differences and preclude a *detailed* rule-book of cities for all times. Though there are timeless patterns and designs-that-work, leave room for experiments, especially with someone else's money!

The big proviso is that the builders and public officials must clearly understand what rules are being broken, and why, and have sufficient skill to carry it off. That's a big *if,* but not impossible. Allow room in the zoning codes to let people try.

WASTE NOT, WANT NOT:

OLD SHOES ARE MORE COMFORTABLE

WASTE NOT, WANT NOT:
OLD SHOES ARE MORE COMFORTABLE

Old shoes are more comfortable. And safer, too. As the mountaineer Lou Whitaker tells people about to ascend Mount Rainier, "comfort is safety."

Western society, wealthy beyond dreams of an earlier era, turns to recycling, historic preservation and restoration, adaptive reuse, and discovered spaces. Why? Simple expediency: economics and ecological common–sense certainly. But if you listen carefully to people talk about these practices, there is also an undercurrent of discomfort with a rapidly changing world.

How does celebrating, using and reusing the old make us more comfortable? The short answer is the term *old shoe*. What could be more comfortable than the old shoe, so long as it was from the start well–designed, sturdy-built, and well–maintained through its usage. When updated carefully—through new soles or modern plumbing, let's say—old things are fully as functional and have the comfort of age. Such old things give us continuity with the past and comfort us.

Our world is changing remarkably fast and without historic precedent. In no other time in the history of our species has change been so wide and deep and rapid. We see and will continue to see great adjustment in social customs, in the global environment, in local geography, and possibly even in our genes. There have been revolutions of consciousness and matter in the last two hundred years. Even when beneficial (and not all the changes have been beneficial) such change can be disquieting and socially destabilizing. Each day we rush forward into a brave new world; the tension increases. Will the center hold? In the past, the man-on-horseback swept into view to provide *guidance* for a population confused and disenchanted by a great torrent of change. The man-on-horseback may yet again ride forth.

People under stress are bait for the tyrant. If we cherish free institutions, then we want a society where people feel at ease and comfortable. Hence it is politically practical and wise for us to incorporate that which we value about the past into our future.

Old things are comfortable. Old things lend stability and equilibrium; old things reused are sound from the simple point of economics. But more importantly, old things reused are a gyroscope to help us keep our mental balance. Old things act as a flywheel. Their familiarity and comfort provide inertia and help us keep our sense of ourselves in a world which seems to reel so rapidly as to spin us off into chaos.

> **...old things reused are a gyroscope to help us keep our mental balance.**

DISCOVERED SPACES

The natural operation of capitalist economies draws out and brings to use all sorts of under-used resources. Out of quest for personal gain, the odd and awkward space—once thought useless—can be brought to life and made fruitful—with enlightened planning.

CONSIDER THE ALLEY
(AS A RETAIL STREET)

This alley is more than alley; it is a thoroughfare all its own. When market demand permits, discover it and allow shops to front on the alley. This will promote pedestrian traffic.

ALLOW ALLEY HOUSES
(FOR ECONOMY AND SAFETY)

The housing market is varied and there is demand for dwellings of many sizes. One way to increase the housing stock (and hence put a damper on prices) is to allow "in-law" apartments: small secondary dwellings on the same lot as a house.

Neighborhood opposition intrudes. For most people the purchase of a single-family home is a genuine achievement and major investment. They fear that renters in the neighborhood will mean a lowering of its quality. Part of the solution is design that respects single-family scale.

But increased safety is a benefit of alley-houses. Police do not like alleys because the natural surveillance necessary for safety is missing. Houses do not orient to it and there is no constant presence to keep an eye on things. But small dwellings add eyes to the alley.

PIKE PLACE MARKET, SEATTLE, PHOTO BY BARBARA GRAY

VANCOUVER, B.C.

PULTENEY BRIDGE, BATH, ENGLAND

PLACE SHOPS ON BRIDGES

This bridge shows mixed-use from an earlier era. Of course no one could claim that putting shops on bridges is a necessity for a comfortable city but it is a whimsical example of discovered space.

The logic and efficiency of putting shops at a crossroads of that type is impeccable. A bridge across a river is a strategic place and funnels people to cross that barrier from a broad hinterland; then to be able to float goods up and down the watercourse to that crossroads is an additional twist. Then put shops as close to the 100% location as possible.

The story of the Pulteney Bridge is more familiar. It is the 18th century. Two brothers own land across from Bath and wish to develop it. Inspired by the Ponte Vecchio in Florence, they finance a bridge to provide access and build shops on it to add a bit of Continental glamour.

New
Retail
Addition

OLD SEAFIRST BUILDING, SEATTLE

RECLAIM THE 'INTERNATIONAL STYLE' PLAZA

Unfortunately we still follow the well-meaning but misguided fashion of the 'International Style;' our codes offer extra building allowance to the developer who creates a plaza in front of an office tower. Granted, some recent plazas were well-designed from the start, but the world is full of empty, windswept plazas (orphans of the 1950s and '60s) waiting to be filled up with uses which might create a richer and more humane environment.

The good news is that private and public interests flow together here. Filling up those barren plazas can recreate a streetscape for the walker and increases economic value for the building owner. Witness these new retail spaces at the right of the picture. They are a welcome 1980s addition to a 1965 building. One can quibble that the building owners should have gone farther but this is a good start.

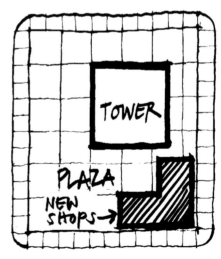

TURN LEFTOVERS INTO PARKS

"Street ends" are places where the public right-of-way runs into an impassable barrier, such as a lake or steep hill. What remains is an urban leftover. But these street ends, particularly when on the water, are ideal for little parks.

Why are there 'street ends' at all? As recently as 1900 boats were often the quickest and most reliable way to get around. Earlier society desired and expected to enlarge the street grid by filling the shallows at the water's edge to create more usable land. More shoreline access was an economic advantage. But as economic patterns changed, rather than using the shoreline for commerce we discovered that street ends make ideal parks. Because such efforts are small, they are ideal for neighbor-hood action. The very first such street end parks on this lake were built by neighborhood volunteers.

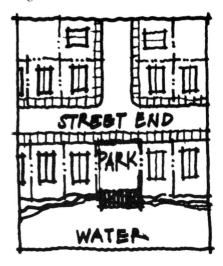

LAKE UNION, SEATTLE

BRIDGE FREEWAYS TO RE-LINK NEIGHBORHOODS

We used to think that we lived in a *cowboy economy* in which we had unlimited resources. Even land was considered cheap. With enormous suburban farms waiting for houses, urban land had little special value. The great adjustment of the last thirty years is that we now see ourselves on a planet of great but finite resources. We recognize that we have a *spaceship economy* in which there is no such thing as *garbage* but only raw materials for reuse.

The airspace above freeways is an enormous pool of undiscovered space, though due to the layers of government involved, tapping it is complex. As urban society implodes upon itself, these air rights over freeways are recognized as a valuable resource.

When Interstate 5 was run through Seattle in the 1960s it was done with little regard to neighborhood impact. It became a noxious canyon, dividing what were once coherent neighborhoods. This convention center and adjoining park were built over the freeway in an attempt to knit back the central business district with an adjoining residential neighborhood.

SMALL RETAIL SPACES WORK WELL

CAPITOL HILL, SEATTLE

This tiny retail space was built in response to a land use code which required separating the building's parking garage from the sidewalk. The garage would have ordinarily been hidden by a blank wall, adding nothing and subtracting much, but the code wisely offered the option of a small storefront.

This space is instructive. At most four feet deep it still provides a place for someone to make a living. An even more viable space for year-round use might be 10 feet deep, the width of a parking space.

USE ROOFS FOR PLAY

Using the roof for activity creates problems for the designer and roofer but considering the price of urban land, it may be a worthwhile investment.

WESTERN AVENUE, SEATTLE, PHOTO BY BARBARA GRAY

SEATTLE COMMUNITY COLLEGE PARKING GARAGE, SEATTLE, PHOTO BY BARBARA GRAY

BRING DEAD CORNERS TO LIFE

Corners of a parking garage are generally unusable for parking anyway, dead corners to parking garage designers. The most efficient layout for stalls generally leaves a parking space which cannot be used (at least not according to the building code).

But this space is ideal for small shops such as espresso, flowers, and pizza. Such retail spaces at each corner of this garage give life to the street and interest to the building..

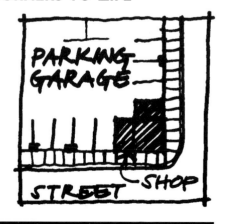

BELLTOWN, SEATTLE

USE SIDEYARDS FOR SEATING

This sideyard had been used for automobile parking, but it was on the sunny south side of the building and so was a natural for outside seating. Note the chips where the wall was cut to create access to the cafe through the courtyard.

It need not take a large quantity of room to create a pleasant space. In fact the intimacy of the space is part of its charm.

USE THE AIR WELL AS A GARDEN

For apartment dwellers or office workers the parking garage may be more important to the way they experience a building than the formal, pedestrian entry on the sidewalk. Their daily to-and-fro begins and ends where they park the car and they may rarely see the lobby.

Yet we give little attention to parking garage design except for narrow technical issues of automobile maneuvering such as aisle widths, turning radii, and ventilation.

Building codes often require some sort of continuous fresh air in underground parking garages. Here, the builder created air wells, cutouts in the land as it runs up against the building. It was cheaper than mechanical ventilation by fans, and more pleasant. It created an opportunity to make parking one's car just a little more civil.

Two other practical benefits:

•Calls for help might be heard on the sidewalk and in the apartments above;

•Light and air are brought to the lowest level.

AIRWELL/
LIGHT WELL/
PLANTER

BELOW-GRADE
PARKING

Habitat Restoration

The environmental movement has matured in the last thirty years. It now recognizes that the preservation of a particular landscape or one endangered species is insufficient. The challenge is to save entire ecosystems. And such preservation is moving beyond mere stopgap salvation to *restoration*.

Nigel Calder's *Eden Was No Garden* describes a future society whose entire culture focuses on restoring degraded lands to wilderness. The political will for such widespread restoration was to be based on our ancient heritage as hunters. Hunting and fishing enthusiasts could be numerous allies for greens even though blood-sport has little place in current environmentalism. It is an intriguing political calculus.

Daylight the Buried Creek

Habitat restoration in cities may seem a barren field. But possibilities exist, particularly with streams.

Under every city are many streams that once ran free. For centuries, surface drainage was viewed as much a nuisance as a blessing. Streams were often routed to run underground in culverts, or if left on the surface, used as nothing but a drainage ditch.

Daylighting—as in being reborn—is basically the process of reviving degraded watercourses by uncovering them. The creek shown here had been a drainage ditch until the designers of a new park saw the opportunity to resurrect it.

Renton, Washington

Exploratorium, San Francisco

Washington, D.C.

Whistler, B.C.

Make Recycling Second Nature

The hardest step of recycling is the first one: separating items of different categories just before they become *garbage*. Recycling at home and work has become common. These devices start to make the recycling habit sec-ond-nature in public, too.

There's no reason why items such as museum guides and theatre programs cannot be reused. Even such mundane recycling gets people into thinking about where things go.

GETTING AROUND

GETTING AROUND

It is a cliche that we North Americans are a "people on the move." Mobility is one of the central values of U.S. culture. The right to travel is built into our constitutional bedrock; the 'road movie' is part of our film tradition. We like to be able to move around, to see things. Some say that this desire for physical mobility is the result of decreasing social mobility. Others say that we are living out genetic directions given to us by our nomadic ancestors.

In any case, the fact is we love our cars. And our boats and trains and planes and bicycles. Indeed, many of our sports involve the sensations of being in motion: skiing, sailing, flying, riding horses, kayaking, running, even walking; and some particularly involve wheels: cycling, rollerblading, mountain biking, skateboarding, and of course, driving. We love motion with simple animal joy.

Any transportation policy which does not take into account our cultural proclivity and pleasure in motion is doomed to fail.

It seems we love the journey as much as reaching the destination. Transportation is a pleasure as well as a need. The Sunday drive to-be-in-motion and to see is *not* on the wane; it is an American legacy which spans the generations. Any transportation policy which does not take into account our cultural proclivity and pleasure in motion is doomed to fail.

Of course the ostensible reason to "get around" is to meet people, for either love or money.

A comfortable city will allow quick and safe transportation for people of all income levels to and from any point without noise, danger and pollution and without destroying city neighborhoods and rural landscape. It will permit several modes of transportation to exist. By this standard, however, there are no comfortable cities in the U.S. A great challenge to creating an urban village is moving people and goods in and out of it.

If there is one planning dogma held by many, it is that there is a panacea for the transportation problems of creating cities of comfort—and it is rail. In fact the belief in rail approaches an article of faith. There are plans for multi-billion dollar heavy rail systems. But these calls may be as much wishful thinking as anything; the effectiveness of these systems is increasingly under question.

That is not to say that rail transit might not have some very important role. Light-rail systems in particular have enormous potential. Small spurs can be cut and fit into an existing urban fabric, be useful, prove themselves and thus systems can grow incrementally.

But this book is not about the merits or demerits of any particular transportation policy. With a few exceptions, it is devoted to showing relatively small things that can be done in six months from now, a year or five years from now. (Bridging freeways is probably the most complex item in this book and should be able to be done in five or so years—even simple things take time these days).

Cars have wrought great destruction to our cities. But, starting from our current context, there is nothing magic about rail either. The job of building a rail system can be botched. Its success will depend on careful detail work. If a planning authority can't do that now with streets—which seems the case—why will it be able to do it with rail? What will likely be ignored—as is typical with enormous capital projects of any kind—is the fine grain finish work to make it comfortable. In fact the hot debate over rail vs. buses vs. cars vs. heavy-rail vs. elevated monorail vs. light-rail typically proceeds with little attention to *how* things are to be done.

I fear that such debates over the wisdom of building rails systems will take the place of truly discussing the built environment and deter us from dealing with the thousands of small things we can do *now* and in a few years to build better cities. We will plan to buy a fire truck while Rome burns.

...we still all drive too fast for the posted limits. We do it because the roads are designed to encourage us to do so.

TRAFFIC CALMING

Along with contextualism in the design of buildings, the most significant new idea in city planning in the last 30 years is *traffic calming*.

Traffic calming is a set of techniques of street design. It involves a variety of small modifications to street geometry and dimensions to accommodate the automobile and to give the pedestrian psychological precedence.

These techniques assume—as Buckminster Fuller did— that we should *reform the environment, not the person*. Rather than modifying human behavior, Fuller suggested that it is far easier to to get people to act differently by redesigning their environment rather than by persuading them with exhortations and even penalties.

Traffic calming also recognizes that the car will not wither away. It is too popular, and indeed, too sensible to disappear. Here is an instrument that gives people personal autonomy over their own lives, their own daily to-and-fro. People struggle for freedom and the car is a very real means to use it. The car will not disappear without authoritarian rule.

But too many cars leads to uncomfortable cities. The person as driver overwhelms the very same person as walker. The real icon of America should be Janus, the god with two identities:

the one the driver, the other the walker, at war with itself. Some form of peaceful coexistence between our personas as driver and walker must be found.

Consider the annoying and dangerous phenomenon of speeding. Ninety years after the first speeding regulations, and who knows how many speed-limit signs and speeding tickets later, very many of us still drive beyond the posted limits. We do it because the roads are designed to allow us to do so. There is a natural speed for any given road configuration. Many roads are marked 30 m.p.h. and yet are designed to be driven comfortably at 55 m.p.h. because of sight lines, lane width and shallow curves. Design will win out. More police will not. Redesign the roads to make better use of our natural inclination to drive as quickly—or as slowly—as the road design itself suggests.

The person as driver overwhelms the very same person as walker.

Traffic calming seeks to find such design solutions. Its theme is to moderate vehicles' speed, give more physical space to the walker and reclaim some of the of walker's space. Its goal is not to make driving impossible but to slow it down to a more human pace.

CONSIDER CURBS

The basic tool of traffic calming is the placement of the curb. Walkers may cross it; drivers may not. It defines their respective realms.

A rural lane—and perhaps even a low–volume city street—does not need a curb because the amount of traffic is trifling; there are not enough vehicles to create a sense of threat to the walker.

But a city is defined by greater traffic and the curb provides order; it is a physical barrier. To drive over the curb onto the sidewalk is uncomfortable for the driver, hard on the car's mechanics and an outrage to social niceties.

The curb—apparently an insignificant line —has a large part in defining how we experience the city.

NANTUCKET, MASSACHUSETTS

BALLARD, SEATTLE, PHOTO BY BARBARA GRAY

BULB THE CORNER FOR MORE PEDESTRIAN SPACE

As with the 'horseshoe that cost the battle,' the struggle for urban space between walker and driver turns on a detail: the placement of the curb.

Moving the curb out into the roadway creates a 'curb bulb.' It is a superior and more comfortable spot for the walker crossing the street. It widens the sidewalk. It reduces the distance which pedestrians must cross and makes them more prominent and visible to drivers. It takes back road from the driver and gives it to the walker.

Though largely made of concrete, the urban environment is really very plastic. Reshaping the curb line has a large effect on our use of the street.

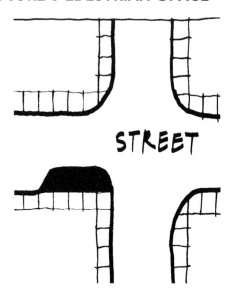

STREET

DECREASE THE TURNING RADIUS

The various codes of city planners and city engineers, with their standards and requirements, form a 'genetic–code,' a set of instructions to direct future growth.

These infinitesimal elements of a city's street engineering code have a large influence on our behavior as drivers and pedestrians. One key code standard is the "turning radius" of the curb at intersections.

This turning radius is determined by the placement of the curb and is the size of the circle which will fit in the corner. The smaller the circle's radius, the sharper the turn. The sharper the turn, the slower one must drive.

Typically, in a residential subdivision, the standard will be 25 feet. But by reducing this radius to 15 feet, the engineer still allows free auto movement but signals to the driver that a slower speed is appropriate.

In addition, the narrower curve places the pedestrian closer to the goal: across the street.

The sharper the turn, the slower one must drive.

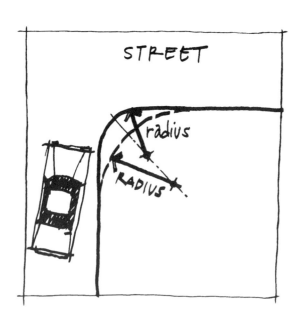

STREET

radius

RADIUS

MAKE BLOCKS SHORT

The short block (less than 240 feet or so) is a traffic-calming device of the first order. Short blocks mean more intersections. More intersections mean more places where cars must stop, thus lowering average auto speed. Short blocks also create more opportunities for walkers to cross the street. The short block is more interesting for walkers. A journey seems quicker, livelier and more eventful when punctuated by crossing streets.

There's an economic attraction to short blocks: more corners. From a real estate value perspective, the corner is the best place to be: it has frontage on two streets, hence more visibility. Its *corner-ness* also provides greater flexibility for site planning, which is the very first and most important part of designing a building. The corner at the intersection of a city's most heavily-traveled thoroughfares provides the greatest access and visibility; it is traditionally the very best place in a retail district, its central place, and is known in the trade as the *100% corner*. It represents the highest possible value and everything declines away from that spot.

The value of corners is recognized for dwellings, too, as a house on the corner has more light and air than a mid-block site and is typically more valuable.

Obviously it's a bit late, in most cities, to form a street grid with short blocks; most of our cities were platted (divided up into streets, blocks and lots) long ago. We live with the glories *and* the mistakes of our forebears. Yet we are still expanding into the suburbs, building edge cities and that gives us a chance to plat with short blocks.

Furthermore, it is not very easy to cut a new street through an existing block; one needs to condemn and purchase private property.

However, getting rid of a street is often a cinch. The streets are a commons and the tragedy of the commons is that no one cares for it as their own. Owners of adjacent property may request that the public's interest in a street be relinquished. This *vacation* —what a smoothly soothing term—of street right-of-way is a neat and low-cost way to increase the size of an urban property but often at high cost to the streetscape.

Vacations were an urban planning fad in the 1950s and 1960s, which saw the development of the *superblock*. Here, two or more blocks plus the adjacent right-of-way are combined into one building site. The practice contributes to a city scaled for cars and is a grave error; but it is still being carried out as large institutions perceive free land in the public right-of-way and local governments lend their approval.

> **A journey seems quicker, livelier and more eventful when punctuated by crossing streets.**

BUILD STREETS ON A GRID

Why even mention such an obvious thing as the continuous street grid? Probably because the suburban systems of cul-de-sacs became the predominant pattern of platting after World War II and the grid is not the automatic solution in subdivision. It is now a choice; but it is a choice not often made because of simple economics. Platting raw land based upon a system of cul de sacs creates more lots than does a rectangular street grid and hence more profit.

To clarify further, it is not critical that the grid be rectangular, i.e. a literal ninety degree grid. The important thing is that the streets be continuous and create continuous thoroughfares. What one wants to avoid are dead-ends which tend to concentrate traffic on arterials rather than diffuse it through a broader network.

Additionally, a grid system allows a complex hierarchy of streets: arterials, collectors and feeders, each one with different amounts of traffic.

Dedicated bike paths are difficult to establish and can never hope to satisfy the demand for bike routes. Restriping the existing street space to create bike lanes provides a greater opportunity. But continuous side streets, for example, as part of a grid make an excellent path for cyclists. They already exist and are a less-trafficked and continuous route from here to there. These low traffic feeders can with very little investment serve as bicycle routes.

WEST END , VANCOUVER, B.C.

BUT DON'T LET DRIVERS
EVERYWHERE ON THE GRID

CLOSE THE STREET

CARS CAN PASS
IN AN EMERGENCY

Interrupt the grid every so often. Block some intersections so cars cannot pass. When the street grid is broken, the speedy and sometimes annoying flow of traffic through a neighborhood is disrupted. But the curb cut allows fire trucks and ambulances to move rapidly when needed.

Breaking the grid may appear to contradict the idea of building streets on a grid; and to some degree it does. But both patterns should exist. We start with the presumption of continuous routing, i.e. the grid, and then vary it with devices for traffic calming and visual diversity. The resolution is balance, and viewing streets as a *system*.

AND LET CARS AND PEOPLE MIX

After all the emphasis these days on pedestrian-friendly it may seem counter-intuitive to suggest that cars and people should mix. Wouldn't it be more civil and humane to create a place just for people, just for walkers? Take a busy commercial street and ban the cars and leave it for people afoot.

Such was the noble impulse behind the pedestrian mall. But it doesn't always work.

It isn't real, for one thing, and it's not something you can do many places. It's really inconvenient and while it may be wonderful in theory, comfortable cities are built in practice. Behind the pedestrian-only mall is a theme-park vision of a city, something fascinating and quaint and worthy of a visit, but not something one might use every day. The reality is that we have personal vehicles. The task is not to *ban* them (impossible) but to *calm* them (readily done). Like the Colt .45 of the frontier, traffic calming is the equalizer of the auto-age.

Mixing cars and people:

•Increases the eyes on the street—some pedestrian malls look pretty lonely;

•Maintains or even increases on-street parking spaces;

•Is convenient, will be used and thus creates sustainable places.

Design streets so drivers may travel but cannot feel superior to pedestrians despite the obviously greater size, weight and speed of their auto.

Use Shortcuts to Create a Grid

One naturally thinks that a sidewalk must be next to a road. But why not build sidewalks without streets?

For example, there may be a good reason to develop the new plat with some cul de sacs or it may be already-built. Such a pattern prohibits through-traffic and creates quiet dead-end streets.

But it also creates few side-streets and all the traffic is channeled to a few arterials. One side of a cul de sac doesn't connect with another one. The parent with a stroller, the jogger, the child on a bike, or even the casual perambulator must detour to a busy street to go just a block.

The solution is to connect the two sides of a cul de sac (or long street for that matter) with *bike-throughs*. These can be installed when the plat is designed, but since they take so little space, they would be a relatively inexpensive element in retrofitting an existing plat as well.

Here is a practical comfort test for the design of a new plat: children should be able to visit friends, get to school, and run to the store without having to walk or ride on a busy arterial. Some jurisdictions now require that site plans for new multi-acre developments show walking-time contours to specific places, such as a transit stop.

The bike-through shown here goes through a block of houses and connects two streets. It is a way for children to travel with less danger from cars and it creates urban spaces where cars cannot go, shifting the psychological feel of a neighborhood by creating car-free spaces.

KENTLANDS, MARYLAND

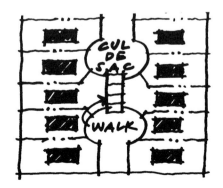

MAPLE LEAF, SEATTLE

SLOW TRAFFIC WITH CIRCLES

The traffic circle is simply a curb placed in the middle of an intersection–a deliberate obstruction in a stream of traffic which forces drivers to slow down. Their purpose is to create a quieter, calmer and more residential air.

Once again, there are no silver bullets which solve all problems. The traffic circle is not manna. Some drivers loathe them and will change their route to avoid them, which may serve to decrease traffic on one block only to divert it to another and to increase traffic there.

Use traffic circles only as part of a systems approach to neighborhood traffic.

Their surface is a good home for neighborhood decoration.

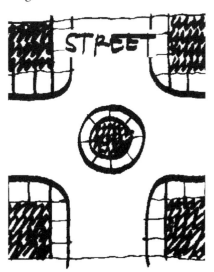

LICTON SPRINGS, SEATTLE

CURVE ROADS TO NARROW SIGHT LINES

Traffic engineers are taught to hate curves in roads. Here is inertia, the most basic laws of physics manifesting itself. The path of least resistance is the path one is already upon; the curve is a detour and takes extra force to negotiate. "A body at rest remains at rest; a body in motion remains in motion." The engineers want to let the car act as a stone in outer space, continuing on its path without diversion. Curves slow down cars. Curves cause drivers to use their brakes. As the traffic engineer sees it,

We are programmed to slow down at curves.

curves are to be straightened at any chance so that the traffic may flow more smoothly and hence more rapidly.

It is for precisely that reason that we should let the road curve. It makes drivers use their brakes. It makes them slow down. It creates a slower and more tranquil environment when the car and the walker have to share the same space in cities. In fact, the new revolution of traffic calming will ask us to add curves in some situations.

CONSIDER VEHICLE SIZE IN STREET DESIGN

City streets are designed for the size and speed of vehicles expected to drive upon them.

A city car need not be able to go 110 m.p.h. Thirty m.p.h. is sufficient for a great number of the trips. Twenty–five to thirty miles per hour is a typical speed limit on most non-arterial streets. A vehicle much smaller and slower than our current car—the golf cart, for example—would be adequate for many urban trips such as the quick run to the store. It would not be safe on the freeway nor would it be comfortable on a long trip nor could it carry a family of any size. But it does have a role. Our city streets would have a dramatically different feel if they were designed for and inhabited by the extremely small vehicle. Very small vehicles would also require much smaller parking spaces, thus in effect, creating more parking slots for a given area or decreasing the size of required parking lots.

But to some degree, garbage and fire trucks determine the design characteristics of streets. That's reasonable. It would be mad to build a city that could not be protected from fire or in which garbage could not be easily removed. The public works departments of municipalities do a scrupulous job of ensuring that such vehicles can get around with ease.

But perhaps they do their job too well. Engineers may require street widths and turning radii larger than necessary and for vehicles bigger than needed. The result is more city in concrete for vehicles and less for walkers, bikers, roller-skaters, children-at-play and plants.

WASHINGTON, D.C.

TAKE A JOG TO CALM TRAFFIC

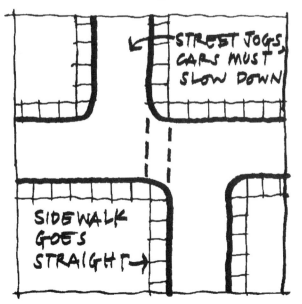

STREET JOGS, CARS MUST SLOW DOWN

SIDEWALK GOES STRAIGHT→

The street jogs, the car must slow; the sidewalk doesn't and the walker may proceed, giving symbolic precedence and greater ease to the walker. Whether this street pattern was planned or was an accident of platting has long been forgotten. But it works and is an example of an accidental detail.

BURLINGAME, CALIFORNIA

CHANGE THE PAVING MATERIAL

The change in texture is a visual and visceral signal to both driver and pedestrian of the appropriate boundaries for each at that particular location. Indeed, pavement in a rougher texture is known as a *rumble strip*. But the texture should be smooth enough so that the older person, bike rider and people with disabilities are not deterred.

NARROW THE STREET

Some streets are wider than they need to be for the traffic on them now or in the future. The excess room in the roadway can be given over to pedestrians or plants. The narrower street will signal to the driver to slow down as well.

BERKELEY, CALIFORNIA

TACOMA, WASHINGTON, PHOTO BY CHRISTOPHER K. LEMAN

TACOMA, WASHINGTON, PHOTO BY CHRISTOPHER K. LEMAN

RAISE THE CROSSWALK

Let the pedestrian cross without stepping down onto the street-bed. Raise the pedestrian crossing so that it is level with the sidewalk.

The extra six inches of height makes the walker more visible to drivers, particularly if one uses a pavement of contrasting texture and color. The change of grade is also a long-wave speed hump which forces the driver to slow down to avoid bottoming-out the car's suspension. In Europe, where entire intersections are raised so that traffic going in both directions will slow down, these intersections are known as *sleeping policemen* because of their ongoing deterrence effect.

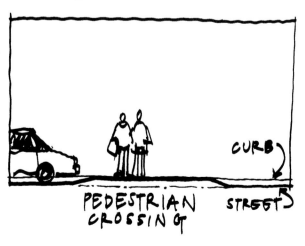

MAKE BUSY SIDEWALKS WIDER

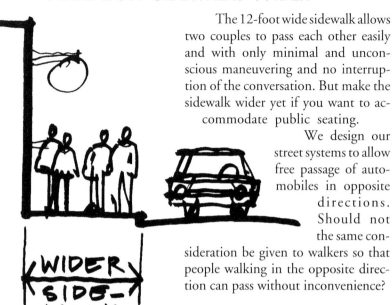

The 12-foot wide sidewalk allows two couples to pass each other easily and with only minimal and unconscious maneuvering and no interruption of the conversation. But make the sidewalk wider yet if you want to accommodate public seating.

We design our street systems to allow free passage of automobiles in opposite directions. Should not the same consideration be given to walkers so that people walking in the opposite direction can pass without inconvenience?

ALEXANDRIA, VIRGINIA, PHOTO BY ELIZABETH KANNY

IMAGE THE HIGHWAY AS A BOULEVARD

In the law, one may live or die depending on one's *intention*. Striking a person dead with an automobile may bring a death sentence if one has intended the death; or, if the act was an accident, it may yield no more than a traffic ticket, if even that.

Our intention is also very relevant when we think of our roads. We may think of the limited-access roadway as purely a means of getting from here to there. But if we can intend the same *transportation corridor* as a parkway or boulevard it starts to have a very different feel. It becomes a more appealing road and provides a sensuous and comforting experience to the driver and the neighbor.

WASHINGTON, D.C.

PLANT TREES TO SLOW TRAFFIC

A row of big trees along the road will cause drivers to slow down. The trees may not provide a physical impediment to speed, but they do have a real psychological effect by looming over the road, and creating a hard and dangerous edge that protects the walker. They simultaneously signal to the driver a place of repose, a place to linger and to glide rather than to rush.

VANCOUVER, B.C.

TORONTO, CANADA

LET COMMERCIAL STREETS FLOW TWO-WAYS

Ever since the 1950s traffic engineers have sought to increase the throughput of traffic in a neighborhood by making two adjoining streets act as one. One street would be made all one-way in one direction. The adjoining street would be made all one-way in the opposite direction. Such a couplet would increase the number of cars able to flow through a neighborhood. This approach is good for cars but not for the neighborhood. The traffic engineers correctly realized that

Drivers tend to slow down when facing opposing lanes of traffic.

drivers tend to slow down when facing opposing lanes of traffic; the opposing lane creates a sense of friction and slower speeds. Thus if one's goal is to move as many cars as possible through a neighborhood, the couplet works well. But if the goal is to create comfortable shopping districts, make streets two-way.

Here again is a detail of great importance to our lives that is so big it is virtually invisible.

Break Up Parking Lots with Trees

One of the reasons parking lots are so unpleasant is that they appear so big. An extraordinarily cheap and simple way to make a parking lot friendlier is to break down its perceived size by planting trees. Especially in lots with angle-parking, there are generally left-over spaces where cars can't fit but a tree could grow. Why these spaces are not used more frequently is a wonder of its own.

Lady Bird Johnson was right about the importance of *beautification*. If one were to do nothing to the strip malls that form the center of suburbs beyond landscaping them well, it would transform these barren wastes into something quite comfortable.

SEATTLE

GEORGETOWN, WASHINGTON, D.C.

Allow On-Street Parking

A row of cars acts as a buffer between the pedestrian on the sidewalk. It also creates *drag* to slow cars. Drivers must reduce speed so as to be able to stop for unseen children, dogs, and car doors.

Merchants also benefit from the short-term parking and loading.

BUILD WITH ALLEYS:
LET CARS USE THE SERVANTS' ENTRANCE

Something as simple as an alley is often ignored, but an alley is an elegant solution to getting the car onto the site without crossing over the sidewalk. Since there is no need for a curb cut on the street, there is also more on-street parking. Streets composed of houses and gardens and unbroken by cement and garages are more pleasant and economically valuable as well.

Alleys are a holdover from an era when there were servants to enter through the servants' entrance. They are particularly useful in commercial areas, allowing deliveries without interfering with pedestrians.

The developer, below, realized the value of the alley and worked it into his plan and advertising which read, "Here's the very newest 'old' idea since *Leave it to Beaver*! We're giving you back your front yard because we put the garage in back—where it belongs."

Ironically, the municipal authorities insisted that the builder make the alley as wide as a street in order to accommodate fire trucks.

CAPITOL HILL, SEATTLE

KLAHANIE, WASHINGTON

PARK IN COMMONS

Neighborhood shopping districts—along with the local schools—are what give character and charm to a neighborhood and make it into more than an area. As mentioned before, it is the relationship of *building, parking lot and sidewalk* that determines the feel of a neighborhood shopping district. When some merchants heard that parking would be banished from the front yard in Seattle's urban village planning, they were concerned, for the traditional view of the postwar era has been that people will not walk and that the *bare minimum* distance between their car and the front door is the *maximum* they will tolerate.

SEATTLE

Underground parking is quite expensive; rooftop parking usually undesirable. A practical alternative to parking in the front yard is to park at the building rear. But this has its own difficulties for a merchant: either the customer is forced to walk all the way around the block to get to the front door or the merchant must have two entrances, which may preclude the needed *backroom* and create an additional door to secure.

On two reasonable points then—accessibility and security—the merchants argued for frontyard parking.

Their problem is compounded, of course, if there is no alley for vehicle access to the rear of the site. Furthermore, many small shopping districts were laid out *before cars* at a smaller scale than we are used to now. A typical lot may be 40 to 60 feet wide, or even smaller, which leaves little room for a driveway to the rear of the property. Where, pray tell, does one put the parking if not in front?

One solution is to rely on the commons of on-street parking. But this well can run dry very quickly, even when augmented by angled- or head-in parking. How then do we preserve and enhance our neighborhood shopping? Merchants are quite right—customers need accessibility. But they can certainly walk one block from a public lot—they walk even farther at the regional mall.

So what about a neighborhood parking *commons*? A lot shared by many merchants in exchange for payment into a parking fund.

Here planners create what individual property owners are unable to do alone. Instead of required parking for each site, property-owners pay into a common pool for a common parking lot. The streetwall line is preserved and yet accessibility is assured.

But there are two issues.

The first is that an overly-enthusiastic parking authority could build a massive parking structure instead of a series of small and scattered lots which *could* be designed to fit-in.

The other is that anti-car ideology will prevent us from taking incremental steps to improve things *now*.

Access for All

The last decade has seen a revolution in consciousness. Mobility for people with physical disabilities has become an on–going concern in design of all objects, large and small. As the North American population ages, this trend will surely increase.

But it is important to recognize that such adaptations in architectural design can be of benefit to everyone and help make a comfortable city for all.

Widen the Exit Gate

Here is a gate wide enough for a wheelchair or scooter or stroller to negotiate and less confining for all walkers.

WOODLAND PARK ZOO, SEATTLE

WEST SEATTLE

RAMP TO THE BEACH

Everyone loves to go to the beach. The water has a fascination for all. These ramps allow people in wheelchairs and those who have trouble with steps to enjoy sitting by the water, too. They also make it easier for parents with strollers, older people with walkers, and rollerbladers.

PROVIDE A MID-BLOCK CROSSING

Some blocks are very long. Their very length encourages jaywalking: a *bad thing*. Interestingly, there are planners who think that jaywalking should be the norm in cities and that such pedestrian use of the street is a sign of a healthy place where pedestrians have precedence over cars.

Nevertheless the wise traffic engineer will channel the urge to jaywalk—just another attempt at making things more efficient—rather than attempt to deny it. The real problem is safety: how to signal to drivers where the walker has the right-of-way. Here, a change in paving and concrete posts with inset down–lights creates a prominence for a mid-block ramp.

MAKE SPECIAL CONSIDERATION

As we grow older, we may not be able to move as quickly or as easily as we once did. Dedicated parking spaces are polite and benefit us all, in good time.

PROVIDE CURB RAMPS

We make great strides in accommodating people in wheelchairs with this simple ramp. But there is also a benefit in this simple detail to older people with walkers and parents with strollers.

ALEXANDRIA, VIRGINIA

WALLINGFORD, SEATTLE, "MERIDIAN ARCHWAY" BY CHUCK GREENING WITH MARE KERN & ROBERT WILLIAMSON

BUILD RAMPS WITH SUBTLETY

So cleverly and gracefully was this ramp constructed that one might use this ramp—with great pleasure—for several years before realizing that it was designed to comply with a law requiring universal access. Such understatement and discretion is part of making our social spaces accessible to all and to making all people comfortable.

ALLOW SHORTCUTS IN PARKING LOTS

Like water flowing downhill, walkers find the shortest path; both manifest a similar law of conservation of energy. Shortcuts are a natural part of human behavior and should be accommodated, not thwarted.

What's annoying about many large parking lots is that their aisles often orient to an exterior wall of a building, but not with the main entrance.

Normally, the walker is urged by common sense to cut across the grain of the lot but the cars are in the way and one ends up taking many small and annoying rightangle turns. Here, the urge to cut across the grain is acknowledged and welcomed. Planted like an

allée in a French garden, this path cuts across the grain and provides a natural shortcut to the building entrance.

Here, designers faced the convention center's main entrance to the street and relegated the parking lot to the side.

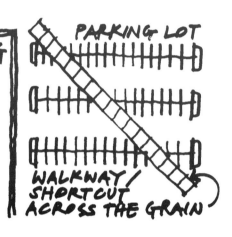

PORTLAND, OREGON

INCREASE SIGNAL LENGTH/DECREASE WAIT TIME

Giving people time and attention shows respect, or lack of respect, as in the expression 'not giving a person the time of day.'

The timing of our traffic signals should give people precedence over cars. The typical signal is set to allow four feet per second of street crossing. That is to say, if the street is 40 feet wide, then the light will be green for 10 seconds. To permit more fragile populations—the elderly, those with disabilities, the very young—to cross with ease, set the signal at 3.5 feet or less per second of crossing time.

Salt Lake City is a place whose character comes from its strikingly wide streets—nine lanes in many cases—a holdover from its pioneer days when a design constraint was the space needed by an oxen team to turn full circle. But its walk signals are very short. Walk fairly quickly and yet not a third of the way across, the green *walk* signal turns to red *wait*. Suddenly the pedestrian faces a phalanx of impatient vehicles.

Another detail to consider is the *wait time* for the pedestrian. The longer the pedestrian must wait to cross, obviously the lower the respect shown. Long wait times—as long as 3 minutes—encourages activity outside the rules. It's no different on the sidewalk than in the corridors of power.

But traffic signals can be adjusted. In an urban village the walker will have time to cross the street and without undue waiting.

BICYCLES

Two observations:

•63% of all automobile trips are less than 2 miles.

•On reasonably flat ground an average person in normal health can ride a bicycle 8 miles per hour.

So 63% of all automobile trips could be done by a bicycle in fifteen minutes or so.

Obviously that's only two thirds of all auto trips, so bicycles are not the panacea for our transport problems. Certainly bikes are inconvenient in rain, in winter, in steep topography and late at night.

That approach is part of the problem. It is easy to fall into the trap of thinking that all problems must have one big and glorious solution. We're always looking for the *silver bullet* and the *home run* which will solve all problems. Consider the urban transportation problem. Conventional thinking sees only costly answers such as superhighways and subways.

But such answers follow from the misstatement of the problem. There is no one *transportation problem* but a great number of smaller issues of mobility.

'Bikes won't solve the problem' is true if you are looking for one solution for all problems. Take into account the negatives of bike riding: winter, dark, cold, rain, steep hills.

Still, just suppose bicycles could be used on only 5% of all automobile trips. Certainly it's not the 100% solution. But it's a gain. Five percent of a very big number is still a very big number. And what's wrong with a small gain?

But we don't have the patience to piece together the many small solutions which add up to solving big problems. We mock them and ask, as one Supreme Court Justice recently did (admittedly in a slightly different context): 'How many bathtubs can you carry on a bike?' Might the Justice's question indicate how rarely he must ever visit a hardware store? In fact, as any homeowner or contractor knows, a very great number of trips for supplies are indeed for items small enough to fit in one's pocket—the washer for the kitchen sink, for instance—much less a bike carry-bag.

Viewed in this context, an approach which might be appropriate for *only* 63% of the automobile trips is worth a serious look.

But the main impediment to making bicycling a practical element of city life is riding safely among cars.

Separate dedicated paths are one solution and herein lies an interesting debate in the bicycle community. Some bicycle advocates urge the construction of a system of *bike-only* paths throughout our cities. Others claim that because such a system would be a new and expensive circulation network, it will be cost prohibitive and thus never be built. Furthermore, they point out that since bicycles are already a legitimate form of transportation, they should be given their due and the existing right-of-way should be redesigned to accommodate them.

Carry Bikes on Buses

One other issue for bikers is the 'long-haul' across the metropolis. Some people are reluctant to bike to work, or for pleasure, to a relatively distant destination out of fear that they will not be able to bike home comfortably due to bad weather or fatigue.

Partnering bikes with buses makes sense. It gives the cyclist convenient access to the larger transportation grid. The external bike rack shown here is simply one solution, and it may not be optimum. The bike must be attached to the rack with care by the rider, who may not know how to do it quickly, which will slow down the boarding process. The rack has limited capacity and exposes the bicycle to the full fury of weather and road grime.

But it is a good start to integrating bicycles into a regional transportation system.

SEATTLE

Provide Bike Racks

Another problem is parking the bicycle safely at the destination.

It takes only a short bike ride to a destination to bring home the importance of bike racks and to demonstrate how few they are: a small thing but their scarcity is a real impediment to use of bikes. The pipe bike rack is simple; it is inexpensive and easy to install. It acts like a wall—for bicycles—without being solid for other things.

TORONTO, CANADA

PERSONALIZING THE CITY WITH ART:

"Kilroy was here"

'Kilroy was here.'

PERSONALIZING THE CITY WITH ART: "KILROY WAS HERE"

I was riffling through my photographs to organize them for this publication. I was trying to sort them out into logical categories. Most fell into place quite easily. But I ended up with a substantial pile of photos which did not fall into any particular category of city comforts. These pictures—of murals, sculptures, embedded objects, and the like—were all intended to be (and were generally perceived to be) *art*.

We are all Robinson Crusoe, going to and fro in search of another comforting human voice.

However, my intention had never been to include art in this book. Of course the objects had appealed to me; I had photographed them. But I had never seen art as an integral part of the land-use issues that were my major interest.

Then I realized that public art is an entirely different animal than art in a magnate's living room, and that public art, too, is about making closer contact.

...public art contributes to the process of place-making.

The world is a big and sometimes lonely place. We are all Robinson Crusoe going to and fro in search of another comforting human voice, another comforting human face, any sign that another person had passed this way before, such as Crusoe's found-footstep in the sand: the first sign of another human he had seen in 26 years—and at first a trauma, he had been alone so long.

With art and decoration we personalize our built environment beyond what we need for bare function.

Public art and decoration is a city comfort because it reminds us that we are not entirely alone. It is a sign of life: another human hand's direct touch which we find comforting in a world of great and faceless natural forces and enormous and anonymous institutions. What art and decoration provide is the comfort of another human's touch.

Public decoration is not a comfort because it is *art*. Whether any particular work is indeed *art* is beside the point. Argue, if you like, about whether it is art when the work is in private. The important part of public art in public spaces is its larger message: some person, some individual, has passed this way before and has put some of his or her life, time and attention into making what we see before us. As town planner Ron Fleming puts it, public art contributes to the process of *place-making*.

Art, public decoration, whimsy— call it what you will—is important because some person has *individualized*

Public art and decoration is a city comfort because it reminds us that we are not entirely alone.

the place and made it less anonymous. The city comfort of public art helps to tune-out the void of aloneness.

But there are cautions. Public art is a high-class form of graffiti, or at least can stem from the same impulse. It is a marker and statement: "I was here." It is somewhat like the running visual

Public art is a high-class form of graffiti, or at least can stem from the same impulse.

joke of soldiers from World War II: "Kilroy was here" which says nothing but had great meaning.

So art, too, can be inappropriate to its location or audience. It can be a

threat, like much of the spray–painted graffiti of adolescents, which reminds us of the hostile marking of territory by animals and repels us rather than attracts.

Public art functions in one more way: as a conversation piece to foster the casual human exchange that is at the heart of the city's purpose. A piece of public art, or an artist's skilled transformation of some otherwise mundane street furniture, gives us something to

Public art functions as a conversation piece to foster human exchange...

observe, ponder and mention. And there is no more surefire way to start a discussion or to animate one than to ask, "And what do you think of _____?" (Fill in the name of the most controversial public art in your city.)

Approaching public art as a conversation piece may sound like the absolute height of barbarism, at first. However this perspective does not at all diminish art but heightens its importance. There can be nothing *less* barbaric than an object which breaks down the barriers between people and leads them into interesting talk.

ART CAN PROTECT US

This sidewalk is directly adjacent to a high-voltage power station. The electrical utility wanted a way to secure the site and keep out vandals. Instead of the standard barb-wired-chain-link fence, the utility's project manager saw the potential. He proposed an art work to top the existing concrete wall that would shield the station and yet engage pedestrians. The artist responded to this clear program with a fiercely protective and yet entrancing 'garden' of galvanized flowers.

WESTERN AVENUE, SEATTLE, "SEATTLE GARDEN" BY ANN SPERRY

LET ARTISTS CLARIFY

The door to the shop was tucked into an alcove and all but invisible. Many customers went to the store next door by mistake. The solution was to paint an image of a door—a *trompe l'oeil*, a trick of the eye—on the wall adjacent to the real door to point the customer in the right direction.

QUEEN ANNE, SEATTLE, "TROMPE L'OEIL DOOR" BY MARCO LUCIONI

BROADWAY, SEATTLE, "DANCER'S SERIES: STEPS" BY JACK MACKIE WITH MAKERS & CHUCK GREENING
PHOTO BY JACK MACKIE

TEACH DANCE STEPS

"Is that the Mambo?"

"Yes!"

"Are you sure? You couldn't possibly remember it yourself."

"...Well, thank you, I guess...but I think you do it this way...then move the left foot that way. Right?"

"Right?"

"No. Maybe it is left...Yes, I think so. At least isn't that what it shows? Here's step one, then two....."

The natural thing to do with dance steps embedded in the sidewalk is to try them out. Certainly these dance steps are *art*. But far more importantly, these dance steps are a maypole around which strangers can string a conversation.

FIT ART TO THE PLACE

A classic view of art is that it should explain and exalt the virtues of those who perform extraordinary deeds; it should honor the heroic. Devoting one's life to waiting to enter a burning building to protect strangers must surely qualify.

Olympia's Art in Public Places program commissioned this work for the lobby of a firestation. The painter spent time with firefighters to gain insight into their work. This work speaks more about place than about the artist.

There is sufficient ambiguity, uncertainty and confusion in the world for us to be able (with little loss) to forego having the artist insist on sharing it with us. Public art should expand consciousness, not further confound.

CAPITOL HILL, SEATTLE, "ICE CREAM ART" BY GRIFFIN MORSE

OLYMPIA, WASHINGTON, "LONG INSTANT,"
BY MICHAEL FAJANS

DECORATE BLANK WALLS WITH MURALS

Of course there shouldn't be very many blank walls in cities in the first place. That's one of the basic principles of urban village design. Blank walls lead to dead streets with no pedestrians and no people lead to danger....and boredom. There are very few blank walls which do not appear to cry out for some covering.

Here an old warehouse was built to the common-property line. In such cases it is normal to have a very blank and very fireproof wall. But if the adjoining lot is a parking lot, the blank wall is not hidden. What better to do than commission a mural for it.

LONSDALE QUAY MARKET, NORTH VANCOUVER, B.C., "TOTEM POLE PROJECT," BY MARK GEORGE

BAINBRIDGE ISLAND, WASHINGTON,
"PORT MADISON FROG" BY BOB & ELLEN GREEN

HAVE ARTISTS WORK IN PUBLIC

Let public art be created in public so that the work of the artist is not so mysterious. It is not just imagination but motor skills that we admire in them. Again, watching an artist at work is an excuse for people to gather.

REFER TO ART

Port Madison Frog is at a backroads corner on a rural island quickly becoming suburb. Like most suburbs it has many newcomers. The island is large and it is easy to get lost. But this fragment of natural glaciation—*Frog Rock*—gives a reference point, as in "Go to *Frog Rock* and then turn left." Or "We're the green house one quarter mile past *Frog Rock*."

Sing in Tunnels

Tunnels are grim and uncomfortable, particularly pedestrian ones, reminding people of bunkers and a state-of-siege. Not surprising: their purpose is to give the street surface to the car so auto traffic can flow unimpeded. Tunnels force people underground and diminish the pedestrian place. Avoid building them. But alas, since some tunnels are inevitable, at least do a decent job of it!

This one, underneath a major arterial, connects a university medical center and an underground parking garage. It is decorated in a style somehow reminiscent of some south-sea paradise. Walking through the tunnel, one suddenly hears the sound of chirping birds from an electronic cage. The surprising delight brings a smile and a wonder. What type of bird? Is it native? What song does it sing? Where does it nest? When does it sleep?

University of Washington Medical Center, Seattle, "The Tunnel Garden "
by Richard Posner with Robert Schneider and Ginny Ruffner, Thomas Gerard, Michael Lord, and Syntonics, Inc.

Embed Things
Engaging decoration can be smooth and unobtrusive.

Somewhere in California

Let Children Confuse Art & Toys

Art should not be apart from life on an altar in a museum as if done by gods but part of daily routine, to experience every day. The artist's imagination can be a good baby-sitter. Build it sturdy and safe so children can play with it.

Madison Park, Seattle, "McGilvra's Farm" by Richard Beyer

Fremont, Seattle, "Fremont Troll" by Steve Badanes, Will Martin, Donna Walter, & Ross Whitehead

SEATTLE, "HATCHCOVERS" BY ANNE KNIGHT

LET ART RAISE A SMILE

In human activity, the squishier the standards, the more ruthless the competition and the more serious the aura required to convince people to take the whole endeavor, well, seriously. The art enterprise proves this point well. But it places art on a serious, ill–serving pedestal which hinders art's great contribution to comfortable cities.

This troll is out-of-the-way, under a bridge, of course. I drive by it often and have rarely seen it absent visitors. Perhaps because the troll is so popular, some members of the arts community look askance at it. But they miss the point. It is *public* art. Therefore the way one judges it must be entirely different than for the private work displayed in a private place.

DECORATE THE STREET'S SURFACE

There is hardly a public surface not available and crying out for decoration.

This hatch-cover provides access to underground utilities and also includes a stainless steel *You are here* button on the cast map of downtown Seattle.

The larger social question prompted by these covers is how to create an economy in which it need not take certified specialists ("artists" in this case) to enrich the visual environment. How can we avoid a dreary sameness in the elements of our streets by including decoration even in mass production?

SOME FINAL THOUGHTS

A Final Challenge

Some years ago I was returning with a good friend from a tour of the East Coast to see beautiful things. We had seen the lovely pastoral landscape and estates of western Massachusetts and Connecticut. We saw the elegance (and grit) of New York City, and the splendors of the Metropolitan Museum of Art and its gift shop.

And then we landed in Seattle; the sky was typically gray. It was a letdown to be back. I started complaining about how shabby the city looked and how Seattle's built environment in no way measures up to the brilliance of its natural setting.

My friend agreed and then, in her absolutely sincere, and comically perverse way, turned and said: "...which leaves us a tremendous opportunity to improve things. It's not as though we live in Paris—what would we do then?"

How this Book Came to Be

The work of Christopher Alexander was also inspirational. In an essay *Cities as a Mechanism for Sustaining Human Contact* he says that people come together in cities not only for the traditional reasons of trade, politics and security but because cities allow people the chance to increase their human closeness. The way to measure the success of a city, he said, is by how well it fosters and encourages human communication.

It is often said that cities are like giant telephone switching systems whose function is to put people into contact. But this is an imperfect analogy; with the telephone system one knows who one is calling. The wonderful thing about cities is that they can connect people who did not know each other before.

Then and more strikingly I found Alexander's small but very rich red book: *Pattern Language*. This book is one of the most interesting and important books about the built environment of this or any century.

Alexander and his team examined the built environment and extracted from it what they thought were a set of rules—the *patterns*—for good building and comfortable living.

One need not agree with all the particular patterns shown in *A Pattern Language*—many people have their differences. But the book was groundbreaking for me because it pointed out that there are widely-held patterns of subjective reaction to the built environment. There exist archetypes of *designs that work*, and have worked for thousands of years, and will likely work far into the future.

Contrary to what is often said the built environment is not all "a matter of

> ## "It's not as though we live in Paris— what would we do then?"

taste." Some designs *work* better than others and each pattern is a way to solve an environmental problem in making the world comfortable. There is much social agreement about what works and what doesn't when it comes to building.

I once served on a citizens' advisory committee. The city was developing policies to regulate building size, shape, and so on. Our group of citizens met many times and I gradually noticed a pattern in our conversations. We never talked about specifics but only about diffuse abstractions. It was as if we were afraid to grapple with concrete reality. Or perhaps we lacked the vocabulary to speak intelligibly about the built environment. There was something enormously dead about our conversation.

I thought of D.H. Lawrence's gamekeeper who said that he "canna love a woman who canna piss or shit." We never spoke of specific buildings or specific landscapes which were thought either horrendous or worthy of emulation.

The neighbor-types spoke—on and on and on— of "excessive height, bulk and scale" and, on the other side, the developers orated about "affordable housing." But there was no talk of real buildings or

....design our land use codes around those pleasing models.

Or perhaps we lacked the vocabulary to speak intelligibly about the built environment.

landscapes, no informal discussion about this or that project, no complaints about this or praise of that. No shop talk about architecture or design.

I grew confused. I wanted to hear specifics. Where were buildings? Where was landscape? Where was the ostensible subject at hand? Was it truly land and buildings? Or indeed, was the subject simply power?

I thought of Robert Browning's Duke who spoke of the annoyance caused him by his *Last Duchess* while admitting that he never spoke to her:

> Who'd stoop to blame
> This sort of trifling? Even had you skill
> In speech—(which I have not)—to make your will
> Quite clear to such an one, and say, 'Just this
> Or that in you disgusts me; here you miss,
> Or there exceed the mark'—and if she let
> Herself be lessoned so, nor plainly set
> Her wits to yours.

Were the neighbors, too, incapable or just unwilling to speak about what they wanted in the way of buildings? Did they have the same end in mind for the builders that the Duke had for his last Duchess?

But then I thought to myself: Ah! I see the problem; we don't talk about buildings. Our discussions are not about the real material city of buildings and streets. Though we are here to advise a government about how it should regulate the way people shape their buildings, our conversations never move beyond code words.

Let's get to the heart of the problem. Let's reverse engineer—let's work backwards, empirically, from *post hoc* rather than *a priori*. Let's examine our city; let's pick out those things which please us and then design our land use codes around those pleasing models. Let's do what all practical people do: copy what works and not reinvent the wheel with each new building. To someone who has never worked with local zoning boards such an approach would be obvious.

So why **City Comforts?**

It struck me as useful that we should talk to each other—when we talk about the built environment at all—by referring to specific details of the city. Builders, neighbors, administrators, politicians, even designers, might find it useful to have a book filled with pictures of specific ways which have already been used to deal in real situations with real and very specific problems. We reason by analogy— would not pictures aid the process?

Our land use codes are phrased to prevent bad things more than to encourage the good. Think of the law as an ongoing conversation in which the majority is speaking about what is appropriate to build. People in real conversations constantly use examples to better communicate their desires. Why not the land use laws as well? They are a conversation between society and individual about how and what to build. So let the conversation proceed with reference to real examples.

ADANAC BIKEWAY, VANCOUVER, B.C.

THIS KIND OF DETAIL GETS LOST

This cyclist is activating the traffic-signal so that she can safely cross a very busy arterial. Such a small detail—a signal-change button placed so that it is convenient for cyclists—is the kind of thing often ignored and lost in the battle over the big issues.

But to me, these little bits of enfused intelligence scattered about our landscape are what's exciting about cities and what makes them work. The real essence of city planning is to be able to look around and be able to focus on these patterns without losing an understanding of where they should go.

HOW TO LEARN MORE

FEEL, OBSERVE, ANALYZE

The very first thing to do is to examine the city in your daily to-and-fro; and pay particular attention to your own reactions, to what you like and to what you avoid.

Examine your own feelings about different environments and your own preferences. To what places are you drawn? What do you avoid? Then try to analyze what specific things attract

...pay particular attention to your own reactions.

and repel you. In particular, pay attention to parking lots and their relation to your destination. A good exercise as you drive around (presumably you *do* drive around) is to figure out the way in which the building and the street are joined. Imagine yourself in an airplane and look down on your streetscape and see how it is organized.

Tours

Take a daily tour. Vary your route to work each day. An old real estate man once told me of this technique. If done consistently, and with attention, it eventually reveals a great deal about wherever you live.

The physical world is incredibly rich and complex and many things will pass us by without an expert guide. So examine your environment in the company of people who work with it on a daily basis, such as architects, planners

and real estate brokers. Of course each profession will have a different perspective but one based on intimate contact with the material. Try an organized tour.

Check with your local American Institute of Architects, for example. Many local chapters organize walks through interesting areas. While many tours focus on individual buildings, the manner in which these individual urban threads weave themselves together into a diverting whole is more and more often brought to the fore.

Real estate sales people can be a wealth of insight, too. Impose on a shrewd real estate agent to show you around; they have a practical and ground-level sense of how your city is organized.

Boat tours are particularly interesting. They reveal how things work

Vary your route to work each day.

from the marine side, now no longer as important as once, but still of great historic significance. When I visit a city with a waterfront I try to do the harbor tour.

Listen

Another approach is to listen to the language in which we all talk about the environment. What do people observe and find worthy of comment?

One of the sub-threads in this book is the importance of the *landscape conversation*: how we discuss our surroundings, the words we use, our manner of discourse. Since buildings grow out of our perceptions and conversation, a very good place to start thinking about comfortable cities is to listen to

Buildings grows out of our perceptions and conversation.

your family, friends and acquaintances. Consider how they talk about the built environment and how that influences their choice of environments.

I believe you will find that the discussion rarely reaches actual things or feelings but is more about abstractions and theories: will rail work? are developers greedy?

Friends' day-to-day speech, public speech by politicians, activists and journalists, and the complex and confused conversation between government and governed in the bulky land-use codes all reveal a great deal about our landscape image.

My Own Research Methodology

It may be sadly obvious but this book started with no outline. I simply started taking pictures of things which seemed significant and that *seemed to work*. In many cases I wasn't sure at first what exactly was working.

Some pictures still lie on my desk. I believe they work and are important in some way—at least they caught my eye—but I haven't figured them out yet. There is great significance in even the most mundane of things around us, if we but look at them.

READ

The Death and Life of Great American Cities, Jane Jacobs
The all-time classic proposed that cities are more about messy vitality than neat boredom.

A Pattern Language, Christopher Alexander, Sara Ishikawa & Murray Silverstein
There are *rules* and *patterns* that work and this book shows what one design group thinks they are. A fascinating book to surf.

City, William Whyte
An examination of public spaces in terms of how people actually behave.

Life Between Buildings, Jan Gehl
A riveting architectural study of the design of public spaces that gets into a lot of (essential) numerical detail.

The Great Good Place, Ray Oldenburg
The first place is home. The second is work. The third place is the social meeting places—the tavern, the coffee house, etc.—and is the 'great good place' of this book.

Place Makers: Public Art that Tells You Where You Are, Ronald Lee Fleming and Renata von Tscharner
Places grow out of *locations*. Public art has a large role in such evolution.

Defensible Space: Crime Prevention Through Urban Design,
Oscar Newman
The basis of safety is natural surveillance and a sense of territoriality that leads people to take action.

Residential Street Design and Traffic Control, Wolfgang Homburger et al.
An authoritative review of methods of traffic calming. Academic but a must read.

WHAT THIS BOOK IS NOT ABOUT

Not About Design as Expensive

City comfort is not about good design as a status symbol, as a slightly subtle way to indicate wealth; and it's not about fancy and it's not about fashion. Good design is not about spending a lot of money and hiring big-name architects, though money doesn't hurt and famous architects may well be first–rate and deserve their fame. Good design is thoughtful and well-mannered. It's not about pretty but about comfort. Of course if it is pretty, it may also become more comfortable—but aesthetics alone does not make for comfort. It's not about visual statements and grand intellectual constructs. Good design is about creating certain feelings of ease and restfulness. City comfort is

> **Good design is not about spending a lot of money and hiring big-name architects.**

about good design as forethought and consideration for the user.

Not About Density as a Goal for its Own Sake

Urban planners are often not market-aware; the surest sign is that very early in any discussion of urban form they will start talking about density and units-per-acre. But these terms are hard to visualize by the citizens whose understanding these plans must have if they are to succeed. I have been working around land and buildings for 20 years and when a planner talks about increasing the density of an area from 6 to 40 units per acre I have no idea what

> **...density is simply a by-product of people trying to be at the same interesting spot.**

is meant without painfully translating those numbers into a specific picture. It is the *feel* of a neighborhood that is important to people, not its density.

Moreover, in the abstract, density is a scare word and hardly persuasive. Certainly, the interesting parts of town are dense. No question. But the density is simply a by-product of people trying to be at the same interesting spot. One doesn't start with density. Certainly one doesn't start the *political process* with density. One ends with density because a place is diverse and intriguing and people want to be there.

Rather than argue for concentration of people, we identify the small things—city comforts—that draw people together into denser settlements and make the mix and mingle a pleasure rather than a dose of liver oil.

Not About Rail Transit *per se*

As pointed out in the chapter on **Getting Around**, any discussion of urban villages is sure to include pleas for rail transit. *Getting people out of their cars* has become a gospel. But this book is not about prayers and wishful thinking. It hopes to show specific things in close reach that can make our cities better.

The debate on rail elicits statements of fervent faith on every side. But I am agnostic, thus cautious. Rail might be crucial. But then again it might not be used. As Walter Pater said: "Style is everything." Rail or road, either system can be better designed than now and neither is the key to creating comfortable communities.

A further danger is that debates on rail—to finance or not—will consume enormous energy and become a thing in themselves: another example of the end becoming subsumed by the process. And then, if approved by the political process, people will think that *the problem* is solved and we shall go on continuing to build uncomfortable cities because we continue to focus on the forest and ignore the trees.

Furthermore, many of us live in settlements where population density is so low that rail will not be feasible—even in the eyes of enthusiastic advocates—for decades, at best. If we depend on a massive investment in heavy fixed rail systems, as some propose, to create comfortable cities and urban villages, we may be very disappointed. We had better figure out how to make those vast suburbs, too, more civil now, and without the remotest expectation of rail.

"Style is everything."

To paraphrase an expression from *Alice in Wonderland*, when the Queen described jam as something for yesterday and tomorrow but no other day, rail transit is *jam yesterday, jam tomorrow but never jam today*. Rail transit is an example of the *I'll be happy when....* phenomenon but on a societal level. It's a way of avoiding dealing with problems now and hoping that one big thing—in the future—will solve them.

So I urge caution. Build multibillion dollar heavy rail systems if you like. But expect no magical creation of comfortable cities.

Not About Government Projects

Urban villages evolve one building at a time, and largely by individuals. Of course the government must set a level playing field of sensible ground rules. But the basic rules needed to create the physical context for comfortable settlements are not complicated. The politics and education needed to let people see the basic simplicity of these rules may be difficult—Poe's *Purloined Letter* shows that the obvious is sometimes invisible.

But the creation of community—fundamentally based on the relations between people—is largely beyond the reach of government and the sooner we understand that the better. Otherwise we'll wait a long time for government (or any other large organization, for that matter) to build urban villages and then they may be named Potemkin.

Urban villages evolve one building at a time.

TO SLEEP IN PUBLIC

To lie down in public and doze in the sun can only be done in a safe place. Perhaps the city has never been a place where one could lay down one's guard, even though the city started as a place of refuge from the dangers—natural and human—of the wilds.

But this is an appropriate scene upon which to end this book; and a hope for the future. One person who read this book in its earliest stage questioned me: "Why put a picture of the homeless in a book devoted to comfortable things?" I was taken aback; I had no idea what she meant until she showed me the man lying on the lawn.

OLYMPIA, WASHINGTON

I had photographed this man asleep because he presented what I thought to be a pretty picture and a worthy goal: a city of such security and ease that a well-dressed businessman (as I saw him) would feel comfortable taking an after-lunch nap lying on the lawn of a park. My reader friend saw a homeless man asleep in the day when, ironically but understandably, it is safer for the homeless to sleep.

That is the goal: to build a city so comfortable that one may lie down to rest, safely, in public.

THE END OF
THIS BOOK

But hardly the end of the work.

There is much more to be said about how to make our cities comfortable, and even much more to be done.

Human beings are endlessly ingenious in making the environment more comfortable. The world is enormously rich with *designs that work.* One of the difficulties (and delights) of finishing this book has been the enormous richness of the built environment. It seemed as if there is another good idea around every corner which needed to be tracked down. So an idea's

The world is enormously rich with designs that work.

absence from this book means only that we ran out of pages or didn't know about it. We can provide more pages. You can help fill in the gaps.

We continuously search for specific examples of designs, patterns, prototypes, and ways-of-doing that work to make city life more comfortable. Simple things are welcome. In fact the more mundane and ordinary, probably the more often used and therefore the better.

Feel free to contribute your ideas and suggestions.

CITY COMFORTS PRESS
5605 KEYSTONE PLACE NORTH
SEATTLE, WASHINGTON 98103
E-MAIL: comfort101@aol.com